Selling Sex

Series Editor: Cara Acred

Volume 318

Independence Educational Publishers

First published by Independence Educational Publishers

The Studio, High Green

Great Shelford

Cambridge CB22 5EG

England

© Independence 2017

ISBN-13: 978 1 86168 768 5

Printed in Great Britain

Zenith Print Group

Contents

Introduction

SELLING SEX is Volume 318 in the **ISSUES** series. The aim of the series is to offer current, diverse information about important issues in our world, from a UK perspective.

ABOUT TITLE

The sex trade is often considered one of the oldest in the world. However, it is still surrounded by a myriad of debates, issues and controversies. This book examines two key areas of prostitution and pornography, considering sex workers' rights, whether prostitution should be decriminalised, young peoples' access to porn and more. It also looks at commercial sexual exploitation, consent and sex trafficking.

OUR SOURCES

Titles in the **ISSUES** series are designed to function as educational resource books, providing a balanced overview of a specific subject.

The information in our books is comprised of facts, articles and opinions from many different sources, including:

⇨ Newspaper reports and opinion pieces

⇨ Website factsheets

⇨ Magazine and journal articles

⇨ Statistics and surveys

⇨ Government reports

⇨ Literature from special interest groups.

A NOTE ON CRITICAL EVALUATION

Because the information reprinted here is from a number of different sources, readers should bear in mind the origin of the text and whether the source is likely to have a particular bias when presenting information (or when conducting their research). It is hoped that, as you read about the many aspects of the issues explored in this book, you will critically evaluate the information presented.

It is important that you decide whether you are being presented with facts or opinions. Does the writer give a biased or unbiased report? If an opinion is being expressed, do you agree with the writer? Is there potential bias to the 'facts' or statistics behind an article?

ASSIGNMENTS

In the back of this book, you will find a selection of assignments designed to help you engage with the articles you have been reading and to explore your own opinions. Some tasks will take longer than others and there is a mixture of design, writing and research-based activities that you can complete alone or in a group.

Useful weblinks

www.amnesty.org

www.care.org.uk

www.theconversation.com

www.enddemand.uk

www.endviolenceagainstwomen.org.uk

www.gbv.scot.nhs.uk

www.theguardian.com

www.ibtimes.co.uk

blogs.lse.ac.uk/gender/)

mdx.ac.uk

www.nspcc.co.uk

www.nus.org.uk

www.police-foundation.org.uk

www.politics.co.uk

www.prostitutescollective.net

www.telegraph.co.uk

www.yougov.co.uk

FURTHER RESEARCH

At the end of each article we have listed its source and a website that you can visit if you would like to conduct your own research. Please remember to critically evaluate any sources that you consult and consider whether the information you are viewing is accurate and unbiased.

Prostitution

Exploitation within the sex industry affects some of the most vulnerable in our society. Often it is a person's lack of choice that forces them to 'choose' prostitution. Some get involved in selling sexual services at a young age and many have experienced abuse in childhood or have spent time in local authority care. Studies show that high numbers of women in prostitution have experienced coercion from a partner, pimp or relative and that incidents of violence are much higher than in the rest of society. Drug and alcohol misuse is a problem for some and chaotic lifestyles make it difficult for people to leave prostitution without support.

There is also a link between prostitution and trafficking for sexual exploitation. Whilst most people in prostitution have not been trafficked, many women and children are trafficked to provide sexual services – 62% of all trafficking victims in the EU.

Tackling the demand for paid sexual services and addressing the market for human trafficking is crucial to preventing the exploitation of vulnerable people. Sweden, Norway and Iceland have introduced laws to criminalise the purchase of sexual services, which they report to be effective in changing attitudes towards commercial sexual exploitation.

We recognise that some people say they are in prostitution by choice. However, when seen as a whole, prostitution clearly contributes to social injustice. As Christians, we believe that God has compassion on those who are most vulnerable and that we have a responsibility to work for a world where people are protected from exploitation and can find hope and restoration.

We advocate legislation on prostitution that offers greater justice for the vulnerable majority by making it a criminal offence to purchase sexual services. We would also like to see greater provision of services to support people who want to exit prostitution.

⇨ The above information is reprinted with kind permission from Care. Please visit www.care.org.uk for further information.

© Care 2017

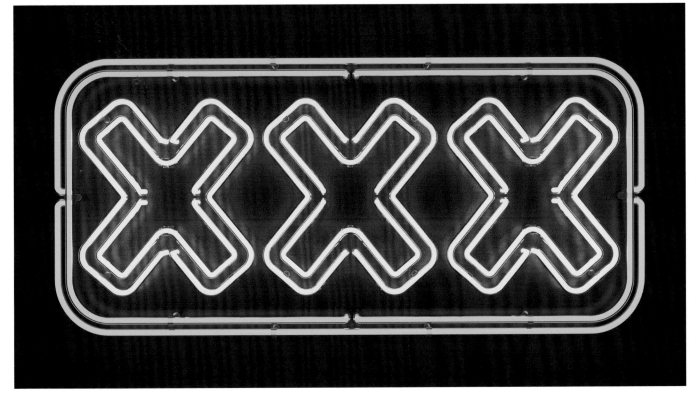

Facts about sex work

There are approximately 72,800 sex workers in the UK – 88% are women, 6% men and 4% transgender.[i] (No research distinguished between trans women, trans men and non-binary sex workers or asked those who identified themselves as female or male whether they identified as the gender they were assigned at birth.)

Most sex workers are mothers working to support families.[ii] 74% of off-street sex workers "cited the need to pay household expenses and support their children".

Prostitution is increasing because of austerity. A 60% increase in street prostitution recorded in Doncaster is primarily attributed to destitution caused by benefit sanctions.[iii] A quarter of young homeless women have engaged in sex work to fund accommodation or in the hope of getting a bed for the night.[iv] 89% of austerity cuts have targeted women. 3.9 million children in the UK are living in poverty.[v]

The majority of sex workers are not trafficked or on drugs. A study of migrant sex workers found less than 6% had been trafficked, many said they "went into prostitution to escape exploitation in other jobs".[vi] If you take into account all sex workers there is no evidence that drug use among sex workers is higher than other jobs.[vii] [viii]

Sex workers face a lot of violence. Sex workers in London are 12 times more likely to be murdered than other people.[ix] It is much safer to work indoors with others but this is illegal.[x]

But criminalisation increases violence. Attacks on sex workers doubled in Scotland after kerb-crawling laws were introduced which criminalised clients.[xi] A 2014 survey found that where arrests of sex workers and clients were high, only 5% of sex workers who were victims of a crime reported it. This compared to 46% of victims in areas where police adopted a harm-reduction approach.[xii] 63% of sex workers said a law which criminalises clients in Sweden created more prejudice.[xiii]

Decriminalisation works. New Zealand decriminalised sex work in 2003 with verifiable success. 90% of sex workers said they had additional employment, legal, health and safety rights. 64.8% found it easier to refuse clients and 70% said they were more likely to report incidents of violence to the police.[xiv]

The average age of entry into prostitution is 19 for women working outdoors and 22 for women working indoors. Claims that the average age of entry into prostitution is 13 years old are based on studies of young people under 18.[xv]

Prosecutions of sex workers on the street and in premises are increasing, e.g. brothel-keeping convictions (the charge used against women working together collectively) rose from 55 in 2014 to 96 in 2015.[xvi]

The police profit from raids, arrests and convictions for prostitution. The police get half of all assets and cash seized under Proceeds of Crime law.[xvii]

Criminalisation prevents sex workers from getting the health care they need. Decriminalisation could reduce new HIV transmissions by up to 46% globally over a decade.[xviii] Using possession of condoms as evidence of prostitution makes it harder for sex workers to practise safer sex.[xix] Since police raids in Edinburgh in 2013, condom use among sex workers had fallen and the prevalence of STIs had increased.[xx]

The prostitution laws are implemented in a racist way. In the US, Black people are 13.2% of the population but are 42% of all prostitution arrests.[xxi]

Decriminalisation is supported by prestigious organisations such as: Royal College of Nursing, Women Against Rape and internationally by Amnesty International, World Health Organization, UNAIDS, Human Rights Watch, Global Alliance Against Traffic in Women among others.

NB: Decriminalisation is different from legalisation. Decriminalisation involves the removal of all prostitution-specific laws; sex workers and sex work businesses operate within the laws of the land as other businesses. Under legalisation the sex industry is controlled by the Government and sex work is legal only under certain state-specified conditions, creating a two-tier system where the most vulnerable sex workers remain illegal and outside of the protection of the law.[xxii]

[i] Brooks-Gordon, B., Mai, N., Perry, G., Sanders, T. (2015). Calculating the Number of Sex Workers and Contribution to Non-Observed Economy in the UK for the Office for National Statistics.

[ii] Home Office. (2004). Paying the Price: a Consultation Paper on Prostitution.

[iii] The Star, 19 March, 2014. Support Bid for Doncaster's Prostitutes.

[iv] Crisis. (2012).

[v] Child Poverty Action Group. (2016). Child Poverty Facts and Figures.

[vi] Mai, N. (2009). Migrant Workers in the UK Sex Industry: ESRC Full Research Report.

[vii] Research that finds high levels of drug use among sex workers has been based on women with multiple needs. For example, one study from 2012 which found that 76% of sex workers were drug users also found 35% had mental health issues and 35% had issues with alcohol.

[viii] Student Sex Work Study. (2016). 15.4% of students engaged in sex work reported illegal drug use.

[ix] Boff, A. (2012). Silence on Violence. Improving the Safety of Women. The Policing of Off-street Sex Work and Sex Trafficking in London.

[x] National Ugly Mugs. (2014). found: "77% of violent incidents were experienced by street based sex workers, 11% by independent sex workers,

[xi] The Scotsman, 16 April, 2008. Attacks on Prostitutes Soar After Vice 'Driven Underground' by Law.

[xii] Data provided by National Ugly Mugs (UKNSWP). (2012-2015).

[xiii] Jakobsson, P. & Edlund, C. (2014). Another Horizon; Sex Work and HIV Prevention in Sweden.

[xiv] Abel, G., Fitzgerald, L. & Brunton, C. (2007). The Impact of the. Prostitution Reform Act on the Health and Safety Practices of Sex Workers.

[xv] For example: Eminism. (2010). and Melrose, M. (2002). Also quoted is M.H. Silbert. and A.M. Pines. (1985) where sex workers were asked when they first had sex not when they started sex work.

[xvi] Hansard (Citation: HC Deb, 13 October 2015, c61WH).

[xvii] Broadly. 6 April, 2016. Why Sex Workers are Losing Their Homes and Life Savings in Police Raids "POCA was created in 2002 to aid the recovery of assets gained through criminal activity. Between its implementation and 2013, more than £12 million has been confiscated by the police relating to brothels,

prostitution, pornography, and pimps. Of this, the police were awarded £2.26 million and the Crown Prosecution Service £1.78 million."

[xviii] The Lancet. (2015). Keeping Sex Workers Safe.

[xix] The Lancet. (2015). Human Rights Violations Against Sex Workers: Burden and Effect on HIV.

[xx] Health, Social Care and Housing Committee. (2015). Sex Work in Edinburgh – A Harm Reduction Framework – Year One Progress Report.

[xxi] U.S Department of Justice, FBI, Criminal Justice Information Services Division. Crime in the U.S, 2013.

[xxii] New Statesman, 19 October, 2015. The Difference Between Decriminalisation and Legalisation of Sex Work.

22 November 2016

⇨ The above information is reprinted with kind permission from the English Collective of Prostitutes. Please visit www. prostitutescollective.net.

Amnesty International publishes policy and research on protection of sex workers' rights

"If a customer is bad you need to manage it yourself to the end. You only call the police if you think you are going to die. If you call the police, you lose everything."

Sex worker in Norway

Amnesty International is today publishing its policy on protecting sex workers from human rights violations and abuses, along with four research reports on these issues in Papua New Guinea, Hong Kong, Norway and Argentina.

"Sex workers are at heightened risk of a whole host of human rights abuses including rape, violence, extortion and discrimination. Far too often they receive no, or very little, protection from the law or means for redress," said Tawanda Mutasah, Amnesty International's Senior Director for Law and Policy.

"Our policy outlines how governments must do more to protect people who do sex work from violations and abuse. Our research highlights their testimony and the daily issues they face."

Policy

Amnesty International's policy is the culmination of extensive worldwide consultations, a considered review of substantive evidence and international human rights standards and first-hand research, carried out over more than two years.

Its formal adoption and publication follows a democratic decision made by Amnesty International's global movement in August 2015, available here, which was reported widely at the time.

The policy makes several calls on governments including for them to ensure protection from harm, exploitation and coercion; the participation of sex workers in the development of laws that affect their lives and safety; an end to discrimination and access to education and employment options for all.

It recommends the decriminalisation of consensual sex work, including those laws that prohibit associated activities – such as bans on buying, solicitation and general organization of sex work. This is based on evidence that these laws often make sex workers less safe and provide impunity for abusers with sex workers often too scared of being penalised to report crime to the police. Laws on sex work should focus on protecting people from exploitation and abuse, rather than trying to ban all sex work and penalise sex workers.

The policy reinforces Amnesty International's position that forced labour, child sexual exploitation and human trafficking are abhorrent human rights abuses requiring concerted action and which, under international law, must be criminalised in every country

"We want laws to be refocused on making sex worker's lives safer and improving the relationship they have with the police while addressing the very real issue of exploitation. We want governments to make sure no one is coerced to sell sex, or is unable to leave sex work if they choose to," said Tawanda Mutasah.

Extensive research, including four geographically specific reports published alongside Amnesty International's policy today, shows that sex workers are often subject to horrific human rights abuses. This is in part due to criminalisation, which further endangers and marginalises them and impedes their ability to seek protection from violence and legal and social services.

"Sex workers have told us how criminalisation enables the police to harass them and not prioritise their complaints and safety," said Tawanda Mutasah.

Rather than focusing on protecting sex workers from violence and crime, law enforcement officials in many countries focus on prohibiting sex work through surveillance, harassment and raids.

Amnesty International's research shows that sex workers often get no, or very little, protection from abuse or legal redress, even in countries where the act of selling sex itself is legal.

Papua New Guinea

In Papua New Guinea, it is illegal to live off the earnings of sex work and to organise commercial sex. Homosexuality is also criminalised and is the primary basis for prosecuting male sex workers.

Amnesty International's research found these criminal laws allow the police to threaten, extort and arbitrarily detain sex workers.

Sex workers in Papua New Guinea suffer extreme levels of stigma, discrimination and violence, including rape and murder. A survey conducted by academic researchers in 2010 found that, within a six-month period, 50% of sex workers in Papua New Guinea's capital Port Moresby had been raped by clients or by the police.

Amnesty International heard harrowing testimony from those who had suffered rape and sexual abuse by the police, clients and others but who felt too afraid to report these crimes because they themselves are considered 'illegal'.

Mona, a sex worker who is homeless, recounted to Amnesty International: "The police started to beat my friend [a client] and me... Six police officers did sex to me one by one. They were armed with guns, so I had to do it. I don't have any support to come to court and report them. It was so painful to me, but then I let it go. If I go to the law, they cannot help me as sex work is against the law in PNG."

The police in Papua New Guinea have used condoms as evidence against sex workers, who are often stigmatised and accused of being "spreaders" of disease. This discourages many sex workers from obtaining sexual and reproductive health information and services, including those on HIV/AIDS.

Mary, a female sex worker, explained: "When the police catch us or hold us, if they find condoms on us they bash us up and say we are promoting sex or you are the ones spreading this sickness like HIV. The police ask for money, they threaten us or say give us this amount. We give it to them as we are scared if we don't give it to them they might bash us up."

Hong Kong

In Hong Kong, selling sex is not illegal if this means one person operating from a private apartment. However, working in isolation places sex workers in a vulnerable situation at risk of robbery, physical assault and rape.

As one sex worker, Queen, told Amnesty International: "I have never reported any crimes such as rape because I'm afraid I'll get charged with soliciting."

Not only do sex workers in Hong Kong receive little protection from the police but they are sometimes deliberately targeted by them.

Amnesty International's research shows that police officers often misuse their powers to set up and punish sex workers through entrapment, extortion and coercion. Undercover police officers are permitted to receive certain sexual services from sex workers in the course of their work to secure evidence. Amnesty International also recorded instances of the police, or individuals claiming to be the police, telling sex workers they could avoid legal sanctions by giving them money or 'free' sex.

Transgender sex workers are often subject to particularly abusive police practices including intrusive and humiliating full-body searches carried out by male officers on transgender women.

"There's a lot of groping and mockery," reported one lawyer who has represented transgender sex workers in Hong Kong.

After their arrest, transgender women sex workers can be sent to male detention centres and special units for detainees with mental illnesses.

Norway

In Norway, purchasing sex is illegal but the direct act of selling sex is not. Other activities associated with sex work are criminalised including "promotion of prostitution" and letting premises used for selling sex.

Despite high levels of rape and violence by clients and organised gangs, sex workers have a high threshold for reporting violence to the police. "I went to the house of a man. He punched me two times in the jaw. I didn't tell the police. I don't want it on my records," one sex worker told Amnesty International.

Amnesty International heard how some sex workers who have reported violence to the police in Norway have been evicted from their homes or deported as a result of engaging with the police.

Under Norway's laws, sex workers are at risk of forced evictions as their landlords can be prosecuted for renting property to them if they sell sex there.

A representative of a Norwegian sex workers' rights organisation explained: "If landlords don't evict, the police will launch a criminal case against them... The police are encouraging landlords to take the law into their own hands and enforce it themselves."

People who do sex work are also unable to work together for safety, or hire third party support like security, as this would likely qualify as 'promotion of prostitution' under the law.

Buenos Aires, Argentina

Formally the sale or purchase of sex in Buenos Aires is not illegal; but in practice, sex workers are criminalised through a range of laws that punish related activities, and which fail to distinguish between consensual sex work and human trafficking.

Amnesty International's research found that sex workers in Buenos Aires reported a high threshold for reporting violence to the police.

"He [a client] paid me and I was about to get out of the car when he grabbed me by the neck and cut me with a knife. I gave him all the money I had and my cell phone, and he let me go," Laura, a street-based sex worker told Amnesty International.

She said she did not report this violence or theft to the police because she felt it would have been a waste of time: "[They] won't listen to me because I'm a street worker."

Sex workers are often arbitrarily stopped on the streets by police and some are subjected to repeated fines and probation. It is unlawful for the police and prosecutors in Buenos Aires to consider an individual's appearance, dress or manners when enforcing a law criminalising communications around sex work in public. However, this type of profiling frequently occurs—with the police specifically targeting transgender sex workers in their operations.

While sex workers operating from private accommodation are often subject to violent and lengthy inspections and raids by the police in Buenos Aires, as well as extortion and bribes, sex workers in Buenos Aires also reported challenges accessing health services, including immense stigma and discrimination.

"We didn't have any real access to healthcare services because whenever we went to hospitals we were laughed at or the last ones to be attended to by doctors," one former sex worker who is transgender told Amnesty International.

Amnesty International found this has led some sex workers to avoid services entirely.

No justification for abuses

"In too many places around the world sex workers are without protection of the law, and suffering awful human rights abuses. This situation can never be justified. Governments must act to protect the human rights of all people, sex workers included. Decriminalisation is just one of several necessary steps governments can take to ensure protection from harm, exploitation and coercion," said Tawanda Mutasah.

26 May 2016

⇨ The above information is reprinted with kind permission from Amnesty International. Please visit www.amnesty.org for further information.

Prostitution: women's groups welcome call for decriminalisation of women

Home Affairs Select Committee interim report calls for decriminalisation of women, deletion of their criminal records and further in-depth study.

Responding to the publication today (1 July) of the Home Affairs Select Committee prostitution inquiry's interim report, a national coalition of women's groups (which includes those providing support to women who 'sell sex') welcomed the recommendations for decriminalising women in prostitution, deleting their criminal records, and the call for a government-led in depth study of the scale and nature of prostitution.

The coalition urged Committee members to look hard at the intrinsic connection between trafficking and prostitution, and to address 'consent' and 'choice' in the round as they work towards making their final recommendations to government.

End Violence Against Women Co-Director Sarah Green said:

"We warmly welcome the call for the decriminalisation of women who 'sell sex' and for their criminal records for related offences to be deleted. The laws which criminalise them have long done great harm.

"We also welcome the Committee's strong language on the need to maintain 'zero tolerance' of the organised exploitation of those who sell sex, which recognises that this 'trade' is different from any other.

"We are also pleased to see that the Committee is calling on the Government to institute an in-depth study of the scale and nature of prostitution in England and Wales, as we share Committee members' 'dismay' at the lack of data on something that is known to seriously harm the lives of so many. Such research should look at routes into prostitution, which women and girls are more likely to be in prostitution, prostitution's

immediate and long-term impacts on those who are exploited, internal as well as cross-border trafficking, and at who 'pays for sex'.

"We agree with the Committee that new law is required because the current 'laissez-faire' nature of English law is making police forces and their chief constables de facto law makers on prostitution in a way that is not accountable to those affected, including local communities.

"We are very concerned to read the argument in this report that trafficking should be regarded as separate from prostitution between 'consenting adults'. Those working on the front line, and women who have been sexually exploited, know that they are intrinsically connected, because at a fundamental level the 'demand' from men who buy sex creates the driver for those who coerce and abuse those who meet the legal definition of trafficked and many others.

"Some have tried to represent this interim report as indicating support for removing prostitution offences from the criminal law entirely. The report does not do that, and clearly says that on the matter of the policing of those who pay for sex, the Committee is continuing to examine the full range of models, including that in operation in Northern Ireland, and for over a decade in Sweden, where those who 'pay for sex' are criminalised in order to deter 'demand' and abuse. The models in use in Germany and Holland (legalisation) have led to horrific levels of fullon exploitation and profiteering within the law.

"We appreciate Committee members' continuing examination of better legal and policy interventions to end the harms of prostitution and, finally, we urge them to look hard at claims about 'safety' and 'harm reduction' when what we know is that the men who pay for sex make prostitution inherently and unavoidably harmful and dangerous. We also know that this harm and life-threatening risk is borne very disproportionately by women who are poorer, women who are more likely to be migrants, and women who are more likely to have complex needs including histories of abuse and problematic drug and alcohol use."

Figures quoted in the Home Affairs Select Committee report published today:

⇨ Around 11% of British men aged 16–74 have paid for sex on at least one occasion, which equates to 2.3 million individuals.

⇨ The number of sex workers in the UK is estimated to be around 72,800 with about 32,000 working in London.

⇨ Sex workers have an average of 25 clients per week paying an average of £78 per visit.

⇨ In 2014–15, there were 456 prosecutions of sex workers for loitering and soliciting.

⇨ An estimated 152 sex workers were murdered between 1990 and 2015. 49% of sex workers (in one survey) said that they were worried about their safety.

⇨ There were 1,139 victims of trafficking for sexual exploitation in 2014 and 248 in April to June 2015 (following implementation of the Modern Slavery Act 2015).

1 July 2016

⇨ The above information is reprinted with kind permission from End Violence Against Women. Please visit www.endviolenceagainstwomen.org.uk for further information.

Sorry Amnesty, decriminalising sex work will not protect human rights

THE CONVERSATION

An article from **The Conversation.**

By Heather Brunskell-Evans, Research Associate, University of Leicester

Amnesty International declares itself to have an overarching commitment to advancing gender equality and women's rights. Against the backdrop of this ethical aspiration, a controversial new policy has been adopted. It calls for the decriminalisation of prostitution, in order to protect the human rights of sex workers.

Sex workers are one of the most marginalised groups in the world and are at constant risk of discrimination, violence and abuse. Amnesty International has concluded the criminalisation of consensual sex work encourages – rather than alleviates – this abuse. The policy calls on states to decriminalise prostitution and to ensure that sex workers enjoy full and equal legal protection from exploitation, trafficking and violence.

"Sex workers are one of the most marginalised groups in the world and are at constant risk of discrimination, violence and abuse"

Where's the evidence?

The policy, which was recently ratified at Amnesty's decision-making forum in Dublin, has wrought heated discussion since it was first drafted two years ago.

Two opposing camps have arisen. A camp made up of pressure groups, academics and sex workers applauds Amnesty's decision. They see it as a victory for a marginalised and vilified group of people. They cite research based on the testimonies of sex workers, which indicates that in countries such as Germany and Denmark where sex work is legalised, sexual violence is minimised.

The people in this camp consider their position to be objective, in contrast to the ideologically or politically driven recommendations of their opponents. Although they recognise that much sexual violence is gendered – that is, it happens overwhelmingly to women – many of them also think of radical feminists as "enemies" to sex worker rights. The argument goes that some strands of feminist research and politics patronise sex workers, and seek to deprive them of their right to decide what to do with their own bodies.

The other camp is also made up of pressure groups, academics and sex workers, as well as famous media figures and actors, who have campaigned against Amnesty for adopting this new policy. In this camp, academic research demonstrates that in countries where prostitution is legal, sexual violence is not reduced – it is normalised and makes it difficult to prosecute men who perpetrate it. They argue that decriminalising prostitution does not endorse and protect the human rights of girls – instead, it further erodes them.

Although these positions are incompatible, they share the common goal to end sexual violence and make illegal the humiliating practices perpetrated by the police and other state authorities on sex workers. The crux of the debate revolves around whether the decriminalisation of sex work reduces harm and violence against women, or increases it.

Clearly, both camps can't be right. So how do we decide which position best protects women?

Listen to the sex workers

It seems obvious to begin by asking sex workers themselves. However, sex workers also offer conflicting testimonies.

> "A coalition of women who publicly identify as survivors of sex work emphasises that women often engage in sex work due to marginalisation, limited choices and abusive backgrounds"

The Global Network of Sex Work Projects (NSWP) – an advocacy organisation, which aims to "uphold the voice of sex workers" – describes the impact on women's human rights of the various criminal law and regulatory approaches to sex work. They support Amnesty's decision, arguing that criminalisation increases stigma, contributes to a culture in which violence, abuse and discrimination are accepted, and makes the reporting and prevention of sexual violence more difficult.

In contrast, Survivors of Prostitution-Abuse Calling for Enlightenment (SPACE) – a coalition of women who publicly identify as survivors of sex work – emphasises that women often engage in sex work due to marginalisation, limited choices and abusive backgrounds. SPACE is committed to raising public awareness about the harm of prostitution, and lobbying governments to be proactive in presenting it. SPACE advocates the implementation of the Nordic model, which decriminalises prostituted persons, criminalises those who buy them, and provides viable exit strategies including education and training.

Rachel Moran – co-founder of SPACE and former prostitute – insists that before we can expect social change in the status, dignity and human rights of women, prostitution must be recognised for the abuse that it is. In her book, *Paid For*, Moran makes a compelling argument that prostitution and its social acceptance is an abuse of women and girls.

> "Rachel Moran – co-founder of SPACE and former prostitute – insists that before we can expect social change in the status, dignity and human rights of women, prostitution must be recognised for the abuse that it is"

She describes three types of men who patronise prostitution: those who assume the women they buy have no human feelings; those who are conscious of a woman's humanity but choose to ignore it; and those who derive sexual pleasure from reducing the humanity of women they buy.

Ultimately, research into prostitution – and the social and political systems which criminalise, decriminalise or legalise it – arise from an ethical sensibility about whether the buying and selling of women can align with women's human rights. Although academic research is important, it is never undertaken from a point of perfect objectivity.

I am firmly in the camp which argues that the decriminalisation or legalisation of prostitution will fail to protect sex workers' human rights. In my opinion, Amnesty International has not furthered women's rights. Instead, it has condoned the wrongs perpetrated against women in sex work across the globe.

13 August 2015

⇨ The above information is reprinted with kind permission from *The Conversation*. Please visit www.theconversation.com for further information.

Selling sex should be decriminalised – but we still need to crack down on the buyers

By Julie Bindel

Those in prostitution should be decriminalised. But the men – and it's almost always men -- who create the demand and pay for sex should be criminalised.

Thankfully, the recent home affairs committee interim report on prostitution makes it clear that arresting those selling sex is an affront to human rights. But it reads as though it is veering towards blanket decriminalisation of the entire industry. This I cannot support.

The committee recommends that the Home Office should decriminalise the selling of sex, and also allow those prostituting from brothels to work together without the risk of one of them being convicted of pimping. It also calls for previous convictions and cautions for prostitution to be deleted from the record of prostituted people, as these records make it difficult to exit the sex trade and seek alternative ways of earning money.

Following the interim report, MPs on the committee plan to look at alternative legal models, such as the Nordic Model (where the sex buyer is criminalised, the women and men selling sex totally decriminalised, and government-funded support is available for those wishing to exit the sex trade); legalisation, as in Germany and Denmark; and full decriminalisation, such as operates in New Zealand.

The report has some commendable findings, but it also makes a few mistakes. It wrongly claims that the Nordic Model is "based on the premise that prostitution is morally wrong and should therefore be illegal, whereas at present the law makes no such moral judgement". It also states, incorrectly, that much of the "rhetoric" around the law "denies sex workers the opportunity to speak for themselves and to make their own choices".

I work alongside other feminist human rights activists who support the Nordic Model and wish to see an end to prostitution. We fight to abolish the sex trade not because we are religious nutjobs, anti-sex prudes or moral crusaders, but because prostitution is both a cause and a consequence of women's oppression. If two people have sex, and one is only participating because they're being paid, it means that one is being used while the other uses.

The pro-prostitution lobby welcomed the report with open arms, believing that the committee is leaning more towards full decriminalisation rather than the Nordic Model. In an article on the Guardian Comment is Free website, Oxford University student Janet Eastham wrote: "If the committee's recommendation is acted on, it would be the first time UK law has valued the voices of sex workers and the research of academics above the objections of disparate campaigners."

There is one thing that both sides of the polarised debate on the sex trade agree on, which is that the selling of sex, both on- and off-street, must be decriminalised. While we are on opposite sides of the fence regarding what to do about the pimps, brothel owners and punters, noone thinks the women and men who sell sex should be issued with Asbos, be forced into treatment for drug or alcohol rehabilitation by the courts, or arrested for selling sex.

For many years I have been trying to persuade the 'other side' – the so-called sex workers' rights movement – to work alongside us abolitionists to campaign to change the law in this respect. There was one brief

moment a few years ago when Justice for Women, a feminist law reform organisation I co-founded, linked up with the UK Network of Sex Work Projects at a police vice conference. We presented a list of joint recommendations to the Association of Chief Police Officers that focused on decriminalising the women. It was a success, but it was unusual. Supporters of full decriminalisation have typically refused to join forces with abolitionists to campaign for decriminalisation of those selling sex.

The pro-prostitution lobby argue that the Nordic Model puts women who do sex work at further risk. Not one scrap of credible evidence backs up this argument.

The Space International symposium on the sex trade in Parliament yesterday laid open the absence of evidence for all to see. One speaker cited Kajsa Ekis Ekman, who said in her speech on the context and history of the Nordic Model:

"Women in prostitution do not have this magic ability to know which of their punters are rapists or murderers, and if they do perhaps they could show us all how to do it."

The case of serial killer Steve Wright, a regular punter well known by the five women in street prostitution he murdered, shows how ludicrous the myth about instincts is. Violent men rarely present as monsters.

Space organised the symposium in

order to give sex trade survivors and other experts from around the world an opportunity counter the misinformation, mythology and downright lies being peddled about the Nordic and New Zealand models.

Last November, at an event in the House of Commons organised by the English Collective of Prostitutes (ECP) and hosted by John McDonnell MP, speakers from a variety of pro-prostitution organisations – as well as a number of academics who also campaign for an end to all laws on sex buying, pimping and brothel owning – made risible claims about the benefits of the New Zealand model and the danger of the Nordic approach.

Belinda Brooks-Gordon, an academic and campaigner against the Nordic Model, spoke at the ECP event. She argued in an article published in the *International Business Times* in 2014 that criminalising the purchase of sex can lead to blackmail, that it makes both clients and sex workers less likely to report violence and that it leads to other levels of underground criminality. Brooks-Gordon is also fond of arguing that the Nordic Model is favoured by lesbians because we want to avoid men altogether.

"One strand of feminism finds [the Nordic Model] very attractive. Within separatist lesbian feminism whose ideology is that all heterosexual sex is exploitation, because the only way to overthrow patriarchy is to only ever sleep with women."

In her speech at the Space symposium, Sabrinna Valisce – who was involved in prostitution both pre and post decriminalisation in New Zealand and campaigned for the change in the law alongside the New Zealand Prostitute Collective – said that New Zealand's own government report showed no

increase in reporting violence to the police.

"It's had 13 years to prove efficacy and has failed to do so. Marginalised people will only report to the police when utterly desperate. Prostituted people don't unnecessarily report their bread and butter. The NZPC claims there has been no increase in workers and no increase in youth but how can they possibly know when ages are guesstimated and numbers are not recorded. I was instructed, and I quote, 'The older you get the younger they look. If they look young they're probably 18.' Sadly, the condoning of violence is just part of the job. I experienced in Wellington, 'Well, you look ok,' after a John had his hands around my throat. Many people in prostitution only report violence if it is absolutely extreme."

Valisce is brave enough to admit that she was wrong in believing that the way forward was decriminalisation. She genuinely believed at the time that it would be safer for the women and would prevent exploitation from brothel owners. The opposite happened.

The committee is right to call for a decriminalisation of the men and women selling sex. But now that it's considering its final recommendations to the Home Office, I hope it takes note of the reams of evidence that came out of the Space symposium on how dangerous it is to decriminalise punters too.

Julie Bindel is a writer, feminist and co-founder of the law-reform group Justice for Women. Her new book, *The Pimping of Prostitution: Abolishing the Sex Trade Myth*, will be published by Palgrave Macmillan in 2017.

The opinions in politics.co.uk's Comment and Analysis section are those of the author and are no reflection of the views of the website or its owners.

15 July 2016

⇨ The above information is reprinted with kind permission from Politics. co.uk. Please visit www.politics. co.uk for further information.

Scotland could become 'sex-tourism' destination

In a landmark decision, the Republic of Ireland has followed Northern Ireland's example by passing a law that criminalises the purchase of sex.

This has several serious implications for Scotland. Firstly, with robust legislation either side of the border in Ireland and cheap travel to Scotland, there is a real concern that people will just travel to Scotland to pay for sex.

Secondly, the Criminal Law (Sexual Offences) Act 2015 will have a crucial impact in the fight against modern-day slavery. Human trafficking is a market that works on supply and demand, therefore reducing the demand for paid sex is a key part of reducing trafficking.

As greater penalties for the buyer have been proven to decrease demand, traffickers will look at neighbouring places that do not have such restrictive laws and move their activities there. Therefore, it is a real concern that trafficking activity could move from Ireland to Scotland.

CARE for Scotland's Director, Stuart Weir

"Introducing laws to criminalise the buyer of sex addresses the inequality, harm and exploitation that is at the heart of prostitution. It also holds those who drive it – the buyers – responsible for their actions.

"Neighbouring countries are now putting in place greater protections in law to curb sexual exploitation; it's time for Scotland to do the same.

"CARE urges the Scottish Government to put in place a law that would criminalise the purchase of sex – this would send a clear message that Scotland is serious about tackling sexual exploitation.

"With Scotland so easy to get to from Ireland, politicians cannot afford to be complacent – this law is going to have a knock-on effect on the sex industry in Scotland. But if the Scottish Government acts soon, it can avoid becoming a sex-tourism destination."

CARE's Senior Policy Officer for Human Trafficking, Louise Gleich

"If we are to prevent more people becoming victims of human trafficking there is an urgent need for legislation to challenge the demand for commercial sex.

"It is not simply enough to rescue and help victims after they are exploited, we must seek to prevent these crimes in the first place.

"If the Scottish Government passed a law criminalising the purchase of sex it would send a clear message that Scotland is a hostile environment for human trafficking."

15 February 2017

⇨ The above information is reprinted with kind permission from Care. Please visit www.care.org.uk for further information.

> **"Introducing laws to criminalise the buyer of sex addresses the inequality, harm and exploitation that is at the heart of prostitution. It also holds those who drive it – the buyers – responsible for their actions.**
>
> **Neighbouring countries are now putting in place greater protections in law to curb sexual exploitation; it's time for Scotland to do the same."**

France criminalises clients of prostitution

By Emily St.Denny

On 6th April, the French Parliament voted to criminalise clients of prostitution[1]. Following in the footsteps of countries such as Sweden, Norway, Iceland and Canada, France is the fifth country in the world to introduce a demand-side ban on prostitution. This highly contentious bill has been the subject of fraught political and parliamentary debates for over three years. In particular, sex workers' rights activists and community health groups have voiced strong fears that criminalising clients would further stigmatise and endanger individuals in prostitution by forcing them to operate out of sight of the police and health services. The bill's adoption marks the final step in a long process aimed at converting France's contemporary prostitution policy framework from one that tacitly discouraged prostitution to one that strongly rejects the possibility of purchasing sexual services and symbolically denounces prostitution as a form of violence.

Historically, French policymakers have recognised three models of prostitution policy. Prohibitionism refers to models where all individuals involved in commercial sex – prostitutes, clients and pimps – are criminalised. Regulationism broadly refers to frameworks where the state is involved in organising prostitution. Finally, abolitionism seeks the abolition of state regulation of prostitution. This model seeks to punish public soliciting, and those who profit from, exploit or encourage the prostitution of another. Without directly criminalising the sale of sexual services between consenting adults, abolitionists consider women in prostitution to be victims rather than criminals.

Until the end of the Second World War, France regulated prostitution by means of licensed brothels, forced medical examinations, and the police regulation of women perceived to be involved in prostitution. The country's regulationist framework was so notorious and well-developed that regulationism was often referred to as the *système français* – the "French" system. However, after WWII, partly in a bid to erase the memory of German occupiers' involvement in managing and frequenting brothels, France moved towards an abolitionist regime. Brothels were closed in 1946, and the transition was completed in 1960 when the country ratified the 1949 United Nations Convention for the Suppression of the Traffic in Persons and of the Exploitation of the Prostitution of Others.

Since then, France has operated a two-pillar prostitution policy framework. The first pillar concerns the criminalisation of the exploitation of the prostitution of others. This includes brothel keeping, pimping and profiting in any way from another person's involvement in prostitution. The second pillar concerns the provision of social support to individuals involved in prostitution, with a view to encourage exit and societal reintegration. Together, these pillars formed a policy regime that did not directly outlaw prostitution between consenting adults, yet making any legal forms very difficult. Moreover, the two pillars were inconsistently and often ineffectively applied. For instance, the first pillar was not only used to punish pimps, but sometimes also to threaten the children or partners of individuals in prostitution assumed to be 'profiting' from earnings made through commercial sex. Furthermore, the provision of social support to individuals in prostitution has suffered from chronic under-funding, with the state relying extensively on the voluntary sector to fill the gap.

The French abolitionist regime is therefore characterised by a patchy implementation of its key policies. Firstly, individuals in prostitution and their families were often the target of police harassment putatively aimed at curtailing the exploitation of prostitution. Secondly, social and health services were under-funded, disparately implemented, and often contingent on service users promising to exit prostitution. Sex workers' rights activists have periodically protested what they perceived to be coercive

and punitive laws that force them to operate underground and limit their rights to a private life, but to little avail. [2]

Since its inception, policy evaluations of France's abolitionist regime have therefore systematically found it to be ineffective, unfit for purpose and in need of reform: it has neither eradicated pimping nor provided consistent and effective social support to those it considers the 'victims' of prostitution. Yet, because of the dominance of abolitionism as a policy model, any discussion of possible regulation or decriminalisation has been sidelined. Consequently, only small changes to policy have been made, but the framework, as a whole, has been maintained. The most notable policy change arose in 2003, when the right-wing government passed a new law criminalising passive soliciting – that is to say adopting a "passive demeanour intended to incite debauchery". This was intended to cleanse the street of the increasing presence of women overwhelmingly assumed to be illegal migrants involved in prostitution, whom residents associated with a sense of insecurity.

By 2010, there was a broad political consensus that this measure had not achieved its intended aims and, worse, may have contributed to endangering the health and safety of individuals in prostitution and victims of trafficking by forcing them to operate underground, out of sight from the police and social services. This discontent, coupled with historical dissatisfaction over the lack of appropriate and effective social support for individuals in prostitution finally opened a window of opportunity for reforming France's abolitionist regime. The result was the tabling of a bill intended to "reinforce the fight against the system of prostitution" in April 2013.

The bill's flagship proposal was to make clients of prostitution liable to a €3,750 fine for purchasing sexual services. Nevertheless, the bill also contained other measures including the repeal of passive soliciting as an offence, granting residency rights to foreign victims of trafficking, and strengthening of social and health support to individuals involved in prostitution. Client criminalisation

and the repeal of passive soliciting proved to be the proposal's most contentious issues. Certain Socialist and Green MPs opposed the former out of concern it would further endanger and stigmatise individuals involved in prostitution. Conversely, the largest party in opposition, right-wing UMP, overwhelmingly opposed the latter out of fear it would lead to an exponential growth of street-based prostitution.

As a result, the bill took over three years to be adopted. Its proponents welcomed it as the long-awaited transformation of French abolitionism from a toothless and inconsistent regime that often harmed the very people it purported to support, into a coherent framework promoting feminist conceptions of prostitution as inherently violent and providing all the policy tools necessary for helping 'victims'. Thus, by passing this bill, France has completed a process of policy conversion that has been over 50 years in the making.[3] The new law marks the conversion of the country's prostitution policy regime from one that aimed to abolish the regulation of prostitution, to one that explicitly intends to abolish prostitution itself.

This 'neo-abolitionism' first emerged in Sweden in 1998, and has since been taken up by Norway (2008), Iceland (2009) and Canada (2014). Other countries, among which Ireland, Israel and the UK, have expressed strong interest in adopting a similar approach. As seen in France, neo-abolitionism is often associated with strong conceptualisation of prostitution as a form of violence against women and/or incompatible with human dignity. The increasing diffusion of this model, and the norms and beliefs that underpin it, suggests the emergence of an international neo-abolitionist policy regime: growing international consensus on the best way to address an issue, reinforced by the adoption of corresponding laws, in order to coordinate action and promote common goals.

While this neo-abolitionism is strongly opposed by many, especially those who wish to see putatively voluntary sexual labour decriminalised and destigmatised, its growing popularity in the Western world suggests the

ascendency of new international norms concerning prostitution. The aim, in time, is to convince citizens, at home and abroad, that prostitution is unacceptable, and to limit the geographic areas in which it is tolerated or regulated. France's journey to neo-abolitionism is therefore not just historically illustrative of the long time it can take to reform ineffective policy regimes, but also relevant for understanding how and why a growing number of countries are opting to consider this new approach to prostitution.

[1] Language concerning commercial sex is particularly contested. Common terminologies include terms such as 'sex work' and 'sex worker', which are contrasted with 'prostitutes' and 'prostitution'. This post concerns French law and policy as it relates to this particular type of commercial sex. Because France does not recognise the existence of 'sex work', policy on this subject is referred to as 'prostitution policy'. For analytical purposes, this post shall use this term to refer to issues of policy and law. Moreover, it shall use the term 'individual in prostitution' to refer to those who are the subjects of these policies, law, and political debates, and the term 'sex workers' rights activists' to refer to individuals seeking to see voluntary sex work decriminalised or recognised as a form of labour.

[2] This is the case in 1975, when women involved in prostitution took over a church in Lyon to protest against police harassment and unfair taxes. While this protest captured political and public attention, it did not succeed in changing France's prostitution policy framework.

[3] *Proposition de loi visant à renforcer la lutte contre le système prostitutionnel.*

⇨ The above information was previously published on the Engenderings blog (http://blogs. lse.ac.uk/gender/) and is reprinted with kind permission from the author, Emily St.Denny.

Majority support for decriminalising prostitution

54% of British people support decriminalising consensual sex work – and the arguments in favour of it are found to be most persuasive.

Amnesty International has approved a controversial policy to endorse the decriminalisation of the sex trade, sidelining complaints from anti-trafficking groups and Hollywood actors. In the weeks prior to the vote *The Guardian*, normally supportive of the charity, came out strongly against decriminalisation – arguing primarily that a human rights organisation should protect people from human rights abuses, rather than advocating policy that goes beyond this remit, and which may even make abuse easier. Amnesty's rights defence is that consensual sex between adults is entitled to protection from state interference, and decriminalisation is the best way to reduce risks for sex workers.

New YouGov research finds that most British people (54%) support decriminalising prostitution in Britain, while 21% oppose it. Men have a greater tendency to favour decriminalisation (65–15%), but women do still tend to be in support (43–27%).

Currently, selling sex is technically legal in Britain; however, restrictions make certain aspects a criminal offence – for example, more than one person at a time selling sex out of a property.

10% of British men admit to having paid someone else for sex. The figure for women is 0%.

Most of the arguments in favour of decriminalisation are more popular than the arguments against; however, one concern with noticeably high agreement is that criminal activities related to the trade could expand; for example, trafficking, drugs and violence (37% say this argument is persuasive).

As a marginalised group, sex workers can have little protection from the law or from abusive customers. Enabling them to be more insistent about healthy sex and sex they are comfortable with is seen as the most persuasive argument in favour of decriminalisation (42%). Reducing stigma and making it easier to rely on police support, and allowing the sharing of information on abusive or unsuitable customers, are the second and third most persuasive arguments in favour (39% and 36%).

After explaining the arguments for and against decriminalisation, we asked people to again say if they support it. The effect is a net four-point shift towards opposing it (now 52% support, 23% oppose), suggesting a wider public debate on the issue were it to be considered by Parliament, say, could shift the mood against decriminalisation.

13 August 2015

⇨ The above information is reprinted with kind permission from YouGov. Please visit www.yougov.co.uk for further information.

© 2000–2017 YouGov plc

The sex work debate

Which of the following arguments for and against decriminalising prostitution do you find most persuasive?

Source: YouGov, 2015

ARGUMENTS FOR	ARGUMENTS AGAINST
42% Empowers prostitutes to be insistent about healthy and appropriate sex	**37%** Expands related criminal activites like sex trafficking, drugs and violence
39% Reduces stigma, making it easier to go to the police in cases of abuse	**27%** Boosts sex tourism, making towns and cities less safe and desirable
36% Allows prostitutes to share information about abusive or unsuitable clients	**27%** Prostitution is exploitative, whether or not the prostitute consents to sex
33% Consensual sex between adults should be free from state interference	**21%** Encourages people to sell sex, when it would be better if they had other jobs
26% Professionalises the industry, giving access to pensions and work rights	**11%** People shouldn't use prostitutes, but seek sex with a partner instead
15% Empowers prostitutes to earn a fair wage from their customers	**10%** Violence against prostitutes would increase, regardless of safeguards

How to implement the Sex Buyer Law in the UK

An extract from the report by the Commission on the Sex Buyer Law.

In March 2014, the All-Party Parliamentary Group on Prostitution and the Global Sex Trade (hereafter referred to as the 'APPG on Prostitution') published the results of its year-long inquiry into prostitution laws in England and Wales. The report concluded: "the law is incoherent at best and detrimental at worst. The legal settlement around prostitution sends no clear signals to women who sell sex, men who purchase it, courts and the criminal justice system, the police or local authorities."

The inquiry also concluded that current legislation fails to recognise that prostitution is "a form of violence against women and girls."

As such, the APPG on Prostitution recommended that Parliament criminalise paying for sex, decriminalise selling sex, and support people exploited through the sex trade to exit – an approach known as the 'Nordic Model' or 'Sex Buyer Law'. This legal framework is designed to end the demand that drives the prostitution trade and the trafficking of women and girls into it. It has been adopted by Sweden, Norway, Iceland and Northern Ireland.

At the end of 2014, the APPG on Prostitution invited End Demand to submit proposals on how the Sex Buyer Law could be most effectively and efficiently implemented in the UK. End Demand is an initiative calling for the adoption of the Sex Buyer Law, supported by over 40 organisations. In order to develop those proposals, End Demand established the Commission on the Sex Buyer Law.

This report presents the recommendations of the Commission on the Sex Buyer Law. The objective of these recommendations is to ensure that the Sex Buyer Law achieves its goals of discouraging demand and of supporting women exploited through the sex trade to exit.

The Commission considers the adoption and enforcement of the Sex Buyer Law to be critical to ending commercial sexual exploitation in the UK.

Policing and enforcement

Enforcement of the Sex Buyer Law is eminently achievable in the UK. Enforcement of this legal framework will also aid in the prevention of wider crimes associated with the prostitution trade, including sex trafficking.

Indeed, the Swedish Government, which adopted the Sex Buyer Law in 1999, noted in an evaluation of the law published in 2010, "[a]ccording to the National Criminal Police, it is clear that the ban on the purchase of sexual services acts as a barrier to human traffickers and procurers considering establishing themselves in Sweden." Similarly, an evaluation of the operation of the Sex Buyer Law in Norway reported: "A reduced market and increased law enforcement posit larger risks for human traffickers... The law has thus affected important pull factors and reduced the extent of human trafficking in Norway in comparison to a situation without a law."

The UK is able to draw on successful enforcement strategies developed by countries that already operate the Sex Buyer Law. During the course of its research, representatives of the Commission met with police and prosecutors in Sweden to learn about their tactics and experiences. The effective principles and practices developed by these agencies are reflected in the Commission's recommendations. The Commission has also been able to draw on effective tactics developed by police forces in the UK that operate an 'end demand' approach to street prostitution. Although current law prevents them from applying their good practice to off-street locations, forces such as Nottinghamshire Police operate strategies designed to discourage demand for street prostitution. Enforcement activity is targeted at kerb-crawlers, while women who sell sex are diverted away from the criminal justice system and given access to support services. Again, the principles and practices developed by these forces have been integrated into the Commission's recommendations.

Recommendations for policing and enforcement

⇨ Enforcement operation: a standard four-step enforcement operation of the Sex Buyer Law would be consistent with existing policing powers. Depending on the circumstances of the case, the operation may involve recourse to provisions in the Regulation of Investigatory Powers Act 2000.

⇨ The offence: implementation requires the legislation to designate it a criminal offence to pay for sex, attempt to pay for sex, pay for sex on someone else's behalf, and engage in a sexual act with a person knowing or believing they have been paid to participate. Being paid for sex should be decriminalised in all circumstances. Parliament should also give strong consideration to making it a criminal offence for UK citizens to pay for sex abroad.

⇨ Sentence: consistent with the sentence applied in Northern Ireland under the Sex Buyer Law, the maximum penalty for paying for sex should be one year's imprisonment.

⇨ Good practice recommendations: In order to effectively enforce the Sex Buyer Law, it is necessary to:

  • prioritise the welfare of the individual subject to sexual exploitation throughout policing operations;

  • provide effective leadership at a national level, including via the Police Scotland

and National Police Chiefs' Council's leads on prostitution;

- take a multi-agency approach;

- ensure enforcement is integrated into, and conducted in accordance with, national and local strategies to end commercial sexual exploitation;

- monitor and evaluate enforcement activity on an ongoing basis, and conduct a national evaluation approximately five years after adoption of the Sex Buyer Law.

⇨ Personnel: Police officers responsible for enforcing the Sex Buyer Law, and Crown Prosecution Service and Crown Office and Procurator Fiscal Service prosecutors and advocates with associated responsibilities, should receive specialist training.

Support and exiting services

⇨ The effective delivery of support and exiting services for women exploited through the sex trade is essential to realising the objectives of the Sex Buyer Law. Those exploited through prostitution can face substantial barriers to exiting and rebuilding their lives. These include practical and psychological barriers, such as the effects of trauma, addiction, and coercion by other individuals. The availability of tailored support services plays a critical role in whether a woman is able to exit prostitution.

In recommending the development of a national network of exiting services, the Commission is not proposing building a system of support from scratch. A wide range of services are already engaged in responding to women's involvement in prostitution. However, funding for these services is piecemeal, rarely underpinned by a strategy to support women to exit prostitution, and there are many areas with no specialist support projects. The Commission's recommendations centre on transforming existing fragmented service provision into multi-agency, holistic support that enables women to leave commercial sexual exploitation.

Recommendations for providing support and exiting services

⇨ A national strategy: the Government should produce a cross-departmental national strategy for the provision of support and exiting services for women experiencing commercial sexual exploitation. An independent review of this strategy should be conducted three to five years after its introduction.

⇨ A local strategy: each local authority should adopt a multi-agency strategy to end commercial sexual exploitation, of which supporting women to exit prostitution should be a central objective. This should be a sub-strategy of local integrated approaches on all forms of violence against women and girls.

⇨ Principles for effective service delivery: while the exact model of

service delivery should be tailored to each local area, outlined below are the key principles that underpin the effective delivery of support and exiting services for women involved in prostitution.

- Holistic, tailored provision: a holistic package of specialist support should be tailored to the specific needs of each woman.

- A coordinated, multi-agency approach: local agencies should work together, via a shared prostitution strategy, to support women to exit.

- Long-term: exiting prostitution can be a lengthy and difficult process. Services should reflect this and work to provide continuity of care.

- Name the problem: local strategies, and the agencies delivering them, should recognise prostitution as violence against women.

- Address on-street and off-street commercial sexual exploitation: women prostituting in different locations share some common barriers to exiting.

- Be flexible and accessible: services need to be flexible in order to enable women living in chaotic circumstances to engage with them.

- Monitor and evaluate: all services should collect monitoring data that supports the ongoing development of the local prostitution strategy and which can be drawn on for evaluation purposes.

February 2016

⇨ The above information is reprinted with kind permission from the Commission on the Sex Buyer Law. Please visit www.enddemand.uk for further information.

⇨ *For full references, see original report at http://enddemand.uk/wp-content/uploads/2016/02/Report-How-to-implement-the-Sex-Buyer-Law-in-the-UK-2016.pdf.*

No bad women, just bad laws – how the laws prevent women working together for safety – January–April 2016

The prostitution laws are unjust and devious and lead to thousands of women a year being arrested, raided, prosecuted and even imprisoned.

Police crackdowns break up safety networks. (i) Street workers are forced into isolated areas and are prevented from screening clients. Brothel-keeping law makes it illegal for two or more sex workers to work together. Landlords, security guards, employers and friends are convicted of "causing, inciting and controlling prostitution for gain" even though they weren't forcing anyone to work.

Below are just some of the cases brought to the attention of the ECP. We don't know the nationality of all the women involved but there is evidence that immigrant women are disproportionately targeted for arrest.

January

Bracknell, a woman and man found guilty of brothel-keeping, sentenced to suspended prison sentence despite the judge stating that "...at neither property was there any evidence of girls who were underage or any illegal immigrants or anyone under any duress."

Bolton, two charges against a landlord accused of letting out a property as a brothel dropped before the case came to court.

Crawley, three women released on bail pending further investigation of brothel-keeping.

Oxford, Romanian woman charged with four offences of keeping, managing, acting or assisting in the management of a brothel. Sentenced to 12 months' imprisonment, released and deported.

Wolverhampton, seven street sex workers issued with warnings for loitering and one arrested. Four men caught soliciting. Three men referred to a kerb-crawler rehabilitation scheme.

Northampton, woman convicted of managing a brothel.

February

Edinburgh, six men and five women charged with brothel-keeping. Charges later dropped.

Sevenoaks, a woman found guilty of profiteering from prostitution and assisting in the management of a brothel.

Kirkby, a man found guilty of controlling prostitution despite no evidence of force or coercion. Sentenced to 14 months in prison.

Southall, brothel closed, not known if any arrests were made. Here

Reading, suspected brothel shut down for three months, application made for closure order.

Ilford, police shut down 11 suspected brothels in the past month. Man arrested on suspicion of controlling prostitution for gain and proceeds of crime offences. Released on bail.

Barrow, police shut down three 'pop up brothels' in hotels. Women involved not prosecuted.

March

Sevenoaks, raid on the premises of a "suspected brothel" resulted in the arrest of a man and woman who were bailed pending further enquiries.

Swindon, brothel raid and closure order against a flat where two Polish women lived and worked. They have since disappeared.

Northampton, woman pleaded guilty to a charge of managing a brothel.

Luton, police crackdown on street and indoor work. One week 48 vehicles stopped and 34 sex workers moved on. Over 30 letters sent to people believed to be kerb crawling. House operating as a brothel closed down.

Greater Manchester, 24 people arrested over one week in police crackdown which claims to be targeting human trafficking.

Redbridge, brothel closure against a "suspected brothel". Two women fined for "putting up prostitution stickers in the area". In the last year 17 other people have been caught posting "prostitution stickers" with some being fined on the spot and others sent to court.

Tamworth, brothel closed, man charged with managing/assisting in the management of a brothel.

April

Glasgow, four properties raided in cooperation with the Romanian police and Europol. One man arrested in connection with brothel-keeping.

Harrow, brothel closure order against a flat.

Medway, man convicted and sentenced to three-and-a-half years on two offences of controlling prostitution for gain and seven of keeping a brothel used for prostitution.

Reading, two suspected brothels raided and closure orders granted for three months.

London, prostitution and sexual exploitation crackdown in Westminster, three people arrested for money laundering, £10,000 seized under Proceeds of Crime Act.

Additionally, the police, who would be given greater powers under proposals to criminalise clients, have been convicted of abusing sex workers.

February 2016 – Merseyside, one male police officer found guilty of misconduct in a public office (blackmailing a sex worker for sex). Sentenced to two-and-a-half-years in prison.

Sex workers have commented about how the laws make it more dangerous to work:

"I worked alone and within months, I was attacked, raped repeatedly, tied up, held hostage and nearly strangled. I decided never to work alone again." (ii)

It is time that the prostitution laws are abolished. New Zealand decriminalised sex work in 2003 with verifiable success. A government review has shown positive results: no rise in prostitution; women able to report violence without fear of arrest; attacks cleared up more quickly; sex workers more able to leave prostitution as convictions are cleared from their records; drug users treated as patients not criminals.

(i) Two of Britain's most senior police chiefs said: "operations to tackle the trade are 'counterproductive'" and likely to "put the lives of women at risk".

(ii) http://www.theguardian.com/commentisfree/2012/jan/06/prostitutes-criminalised

20 May 2016

⇨ The above information is reprinted with kind permission from the English Collective of Prostitutes. Please visit www.prostitutescollective.net for further information.

"Mandela would have supported us": South African feminists fight to abolish the sex trade

Campaigners hit out at the myth that nations should legalise "the oldest trade in the world".

By Julie Bindel

South Africa is one of the many countries in the global south that is host to a vibrant "sex workers' rights" movement, calling for full decriminalisation of the sex trade.

But in Cape Town at least, this popular narrative is being increasingly challenged by survivors of prostitution, feminist abolitionists and human rights activists, under the banner of Embrace Dignity, an NGO founded by former health minister Nozizwe Madlala-Routledge.

A former ANC activist, Madlala-Routledge has devoted much of her life to ensuring women get their full rights in South Africa. A member of Parliament from 1994 to 2009, and Chair of the ANC Parliamentary Caucus, on leaving politics she wanted to put her experience to good use.

In 2009 Madlala-Routledge was invited to New York City (NYC) to give a presentation to NoVo, a women's human-rights organisation, on the topic of trafficking and prostitution in South Africa. The FIFA World Cup was due to be held the following year, and the pro-prostitution pressure organisation Sex Worker Advocacy Taskforce (Sweat) had called on the Government to speed up the decriminalisation of prostitution, claiming that it would solve the problems inherent to the sex trade, and offer protection for those involved.

"Being a Quaker and a feminist I should have naturally have been arguing for the abolition of the sex trade," says Nozizwe when we meet in the Embrace Dignity offices in Woodstock, Cape Town, "but I had swallowed the line about women having control of their bodies [and that] prostitution is the oldest profession."

Madlala-Routledge had already begun to worry that the World Cup would provide an ideal opportunity for criminal gangs to traffic women into and around the country to meet the demand of the thousands of male spectators and participants.

"Almost everybody else was talking about how fantastic this opportunity was for South Africa," says Madlala-Routledge, "but I knew it meant bad news for women and girls."

In conducting her research for NoVo, Madlala-Routledge discovered that the loudest voices were calling to decriminalise not just the women and men in prostitution, but also the pimps, brothel owner and sex buyers.

Preparing for her flight to NYC, Madlala-Routledge picked up a book entitled *The Idea of Prostitution*, a convincing argument against the acceptance and normalisation of the sex trade by the feminist scholar and feminist abolitionist, Sheila Jeffreys.

"I had no idea how it had even come to be on my shelf," says Madlala-Routledge, "but I read every word, and when I arrived in NYC I tore up my presentation [which otherwise would have been far more accommodating of the argument that blanket decriminalisation was the only way to eradicate the harms] and delivered a very different one. When I got back to Cape Town I began to focus on campaigning for abolition."

In 2011, Embrace Dignity was registered as an official NGO,

and today it is thriving, with new volunteers knocking at its door every month, and a sway of prostituted women, and those who have left the industry, coming to them for help and advice.

As well as offering support to women to exit prostitution, and running education and awareness programmes in schools, townships, and for the general public, Embrace Dignity campaigns to change the current laws on the sex trade in South Africa.

"We look at the philosophical foundations of the Nordic law [where those selling sex are decriminalised, and sex buying becomes a criminal offence]," says Madlala-Routledge. "It explained prostitution is seen as gender-based violence in Sweden, and how the law needed to treat buyers and sellers differently because, in the main, women are forced or coerced by poverty and gender inequality, so therefore any criminal sanctions should be focused on the buyers, and the women should be helped to exit."

But Embrace Dignity has yet to convince the majority of funders and politicians that their approach is the correct one. SWEAT has been active across South Africa since the early 1990s, and is generously funded by George Soros' Open Society Foundation.

At the Embrace Dignity offices I meet Dudu Ndlovu, a gender studies student who was previously a volunteer at Sweat. I ask what had led to her shifting positions and becoming sympathetic to the abolitionist position.

"What's amazing about the work we're doing here is that we really are pushing for actually reducing harm, like truly, honestly reducing harm and exposing the fact that there is an alternative. It is a comprehensive view, and it is really the truth."

Mickey Meji has worked with Embrace Dignity for three years, and was also formerly involved with Sweat, both as a volunteer and as a paid worker.

"Initially when I joined Sweat it was the only organisation willing to work with women who are prostituted, except they called us 'sex workers'," says Meji. "Since I was on the street and I couldn't speak with anybody about this, I felt I had found a space for the very first time where I could actually be myself and talk about things I hadn't talked about with any person."

Meji eventually realised that pro-prostitution organisations tend to be led by the available funding rather than concern for those involved in the sex trade. "The big funders are willing to fund decriminalisation of prostitution," says Meji, "and the idea that prostitution is simply 'sex work'.

It is not though, it is abuse of women."

At Sistahood – a support group for women wishing to leave the sex trade, set up by Embrace Dignity – Meji stands by a whiteboard, scrawling random words and sentences shouted out by the 20-plus women sitting around a large table. "Prostitution must fall", "Education must rise", and "Women and girls are not for sale", they shout.

The women, mainly black South Africans, all have stories of violence from pimps, sex buyers and police, but they are also visualising a future free from prostitution. Many are keen to campaign for the introduction of a law to criminalise the demand.

"These men [sex buyers] have a comfortable life," says one of the women, "after they have done with us they go back to their homes and their wives. We want them to be exposed and for it to be known that this is what they are doing."

On my last day in Cape Town I meet Madlala-Routledge for coffee, and ask her what are her future plans for Embrace Dignity. She tells me, in her soft but authoritative voice that the biggest challenge is to educate society and raise awareness about the truth of the sex trades, and of what prostitution represents for poor, black women.

"Mandela would understand," says Madlala-Routledge, "I seriously believe that if we had gone to him to open his eyes, he would have been on our side saying, 'the nation is not free while women remain in oppression, while poor women, especially marginalised women remain in such dire oppression, dire poverty.'

"We are not free, and that's what drives me. I can't really enjoy my freedom and my rights while others are held in the captivity of prostitution."

28 March 2017

⇨ The above information is reprinted with kind permission from the *International Business Times*. Please visit www.ibtimes.co.uk for further information.

Student sex work "must be choice, never a necessity"

Significant numbers of students are turning to sex work in order to avoid debt and cover basic living expenses, a groundbreaking new report from Swansea University and NUS Wales has found.

Nearly five per cent of UK students have worked in the sex industry and nearly 22 per cent of students have considered working in the sex industry.

Rosie Inman, NUS Wales Women's Officer, said she wanted to ensure the financial accessibility of university is such that sex work is a choice and never a necessity. Our research shows students are generally living below the breadline as the cost of living has spiralled and financial support frozen.

Rosie welcomed the wide-ranging report into the extent, needs, and motivations for student sex work as a "valuable piece of

research" that allows the higher education sector and all of its partners to implement meaningful and positive change for student sex workers. She went on to say:

"NUS Wales recognises that sex work can be a choice for students, as the nature of the work allows them the flexibility to keep up with the rigours of study, while funding their living costs. However, we are concerned that so many students reported that covering basic living expenses was a strong factor in their decision to enter sex work.

> **"NUS Wales recognises that sex work can be a choice for students, as the nature of the work allows them the flexibility to keep up with the rigours of study, while funding their living costs. However we are concerned that so many students reported that covering basic living expenses was a strong factor in their decision to enter sex work"**

"We are pleased to see universities throughout Wales have taken part in the research. The findings have demonstrated universities offer a number of services of direct benefit to student sex workers including financial support and the welfare of students. The research highlights how these services are relied upon more by students involved in sex work than other students and are deserving of further investment, particularly counselling and well being services.

"As a result of this research, the need for university policy or guidance on how to support sex workers is clear. Prior to this, there has been no research substantial enough to base services on. Going forward, NUS Wales supports further training of the sector to address this gap. This training must be student-centred and ensure staff are able to support students and that feelings of stigma that students experience are not reinforced. Those students working towards certain vocational degrees must also receive support.

"The main priority must be to maintain the well being of students involved in sex work, not to stigmatise them."

27 March 2015

⇨ The above information is reprinted with kind permission from the National Union of Students. Please visit www. nus.org.uk for further information.

Liberals must face the reality of what prostitution does to women

By Julie Bindel

It seems that everyone has an opinion on prostitution, but few know very much about it. That is certainly what I found in researching my book on the global sex trade. Mythology, rather than informed opinion, rules.

I am told on a regular basis that criminalising any aspect of the sex trade will "force it underground" – something that does not happen for the simple reason that the punters need to find it. I hide my despair at hearing, for the millionth time, that if men cannot access paid sex they will be forced to find a woman to rape, which is tantamount to arguing that men have no control over their sexual behaviour. And I am informed that decriminalisation will result in almost zero violence towards 'sex workers' because it is the police who carry out the vast majority of rapes. Sometimes, those who come out with this rubbish describe themselves as current or former sex workers. The unpalatable truth is that not everyone that earns

a living selling sex is expert in what might be the best way to legislate or manage the sex industry. Self-interest and, all too often, self-delusion trumps sense and logic.

The biggest ruck in recent decades between the 'sex workers' rights' activists and feminist abolitionists is over the growing popularity of the Nordic model as a way to deal with the problems inherent in the sex trade. The Nordic model shifts the criminal burden onto the buyer, removes it from the prostituted person, and offers support and exiting services to those wishing to leave the industry.

Scottish Labour has argued in its recently published manifesto that it supports the Nordic model. If the policy were to eventually become legislation, Scotland would be following in the footsteps of Sweden, Norway, Iceland, Northern Ireland and France. Several other countries are considering introducing the so-called Nordic model, including countries

that have previously legalised all aspects of the sex trade, namely Germany and Holland.

"But you are denying sex workers their agency! Sex workers want rights not rescue. It is a choice. The only harm to sex workers is perpetrated by abolitionists and the police. The New Zealand model is the way forward. If you criminalise the client, the sex worker is criminalised by default."

The reader will be familiar with these arguments, because this publication seems to favour blanket decriminalisation of the sex trade over any other approach. Just use the 'search' facility and have a look at the number of pro-decriminalisation articles compared to those favouring criminalising the demand.

One of those articles denouncing the Nordic model contained the risible line, "Why is it so hard to accept that women enjoy sex and can make informed decisions about their own bodies?" The author, Ugly Mug coordinator Alex Feis-Bryce, seemed to imagine that women are involved in prostitution because of the multiple orgasms on tap from encounters with punters.

I am a secularist, feminist, human rights activist who opposes all unnecessary intervention of the state. I believe that the sex trade should be eradicated because it is both a cause and a consequence of women's oppression, not because it involves sex outside of love and marriage.

No other human rights violation towards women and girls, which is how feminist abolitionists view prostitution, is so grossly misunderstood by the vast majority of citizens the world over. Whilst domestic violence has often been, and sometimes still is, assumed to be the fault of the victim ("she was nagging him", "she failed to understand his moods"), there has been a significant improvement, as a result of feminist campaigning and interventions, in the way that those experiencing it are supported and the perpetrators called to task.

Rapists are often seen as men who could not 'help themselves', or who were coerced into committing such a crime by the behaviour and dress sense of the victims, but increasingly, again as a result of feminism, rape is viewed as an expression of misogyny, rather than one of uncontrollable sexual desire.

In recent years, despite the increasing numbers of women coming out as 'survivors' of the sex trade, the dominant discourse is one of prostitution being about 'choice' and 'agency' for the women involved. The only human rights abuse in the sex trade, according to the liberals, libertarians and many of those who profit from selling sex, is when men are denied the right to purchase sex. The renting of women's orifices for sexual release is not, on the other hand, considered a violation. The women selling sex, according to this logic, are the victims of pearl-clutching moralists who wish to take away their right to earn a living, rather than of sexual servitude.

The war that rages between feminists such as myself, who seek to abolish the sex trade, and those who see prostitution as a valid choice, is fuelled by the widely held belief that feminist abolitionists wish to 'rescue fallen women' and demonise the men who pay for sex.

The battle is currently being fought in the home affairs select committee inquiry on prostitution. Yesterday, Paris Lees and Brooke Magnanti gave evidence to the committee. Both women have sold sex in the past. Both are rabidly opposed to the Nordic model, and, during their evidence, refused to acknowledge the harms of the sex trade. When asked if she had ever witnessed or experienced violence during her time in prostitution, Lees replied: "No, I've never been raped – I'm a sex worker, not trafficked". It's as though only trafficked women are ever abused by pimps or punters. I have interviewed 40 sex trade survivors for my book and over 100 previously for other research. Every single one

had suffered multiple rapes. Rape endemic in prostitution is universally documented.

Lees and Magnanti joined the chorus of other sex workers' rights activists opposed to the Nordic model when they said they would favour blanket decriminalisation of the sex trade, such as adopted by New Zealand in 2003. According to its cheerleaders, women find it easier to report to the police since all laws on pimping and brothel owning were repealed. But according to the Government's own report on the law, five years after decriminalisation, the women find it just as difficult to report as they did prior to 2003. It is a commonly-held assumption that decriminalisation reduces stigma towards the women involved. However, as the same report states: "This appears to have changed little post-decriminalisation. Stigmatisation plays a key role in non-reporting of incidents."

The women in the sex trade I met on a recent research visit to New Zealand told me the law has not helped them at all. The street-based women said the police are still abusive arseholes, and those in brothels said that as a result of decriminalisation the pimps now have more power and legal rights than the women.

The Nordic model is not perfect. But at least it is visionary and progressive in that it sends out a clear message that women are not commodities to be bought and sold, and that men will not simultaneously combust if they can't get their rocks off with women they have to pay in order to get their consent. The commonly held and deeply depressing view that demand for prostitution can never be eliminated is as absurd as arguing that the working classes belong in the gutter.

Julie Bindel is a writer, feminist, and co-founder of the law-reform group Justice for Women. Her new book, *The Pimping of Prostitution: Abolishing the Sex Trade Myth*, will be published by Palsgrave McMillan in 2017.

11 May 2016

⇨ The above information is reprinted with kind permission from politics.co.uk. Please visit their website for further information.

The role and impact of organised crime in the local off-street sex market

An extract from The Police Foundation report.

Key messages

⇨ In a single city 65 brothels, linked to 74 offenders, were identified over a two-year period. Over three quarters (77 per cent) displayed links to organised crime groups.

⇨ There was a high level of turnover and movement of those working in brothels. In a third (29 per cent) of brothels there was evidence that sex workers' movements had been controlled.

⇨ Organised crime pervades the off-street sex market but was not prioritised for a response by local police teams.

⇨ No single agency took ownership of the problem of exploitation in the off-street sex market and there was very little proactive engagement with vulnerable sex workers.

Introduction

Unlike the on-street sex market, which is more visible to the public, the more hidden off-street sex market has received relatively little attention from practitioners, policymakers and researchers. This is in spite of the heightened risk to those working in brothels of exploitation and abuse at the hands of perpetrators seeking to control and profit from the sex market. Tackling trafficking and exploitation are key components of the Government's Serious and Organised Crime Strategy[1], with the estimated cost to the UK being £890 million each year[2]. However, little is currently known about perpetrators and organised crime groups (OCGs) operating in the UK sex market.

National agencies with a UK-wide perspective on organised crime have dominated policy debates on control

in the UK sex market (often focused on human trafficking) but it remains unclear what this really means for communities and whether it is a problem that is significant enough to merit more attention from local practitioners. To address this gap in knowledge, this study took a ground-floor view of the off-street sex market within a single city, with the aim of assessing:

⇨ How much of the off-street sex market is controlled by OCGs and what this looks like.

⇨ The impact it has in local communities.

⇨ The response (including key challenges) from the police and other local agencies.

The scale of the adult sex market controlled by organised crime

A total of 65 brothels were identified as operating in the city during 2013 and 2014, linked to 142 sex workers and 74 offenders who owned or helped to manage them. This reflects only the information recorded in the crime and intelligence databases and it is known much of the adult sex market goes unregistered by the police, so the actual number will inevitably be much higher.

The business-like structures required to manage brothels so they are profitable and avoid police attention are strong grounds to presume a link to organised crime[3]. Nearly half of brothels were managed by more than one offender (49 per cent). A third (32 per cent) were run by offenders who also managed other brothels and a similar proportion (29 per cent) had links to other types of organised criminality, predominantly drug supply.

Human trafficking is a serious

and often complex crime, and is a prominent feature in the UK Serious and Organised Crime Strategy[4]. For this reason trafficking was adopted as an indicator for the involvement of organised crime in the sex market. Our analysis suggests the movement and recruitment of sex workers was controlled in one third (29 per cent) of brothels. Additionally, nearly half of the identified brothels (45 per cent) were linked to sex workers who moved between different brothels (the extent of control and coordination of these movements was unclear).

What does it look like in communities?

The 65 brothels took one of three distinct forms:

Residential brothels

38 brothels were known to the police and located in addresses indistinguishable from all others, often in deprived residential estates. A third (34 per cent) of known sex workers and nearly two-thirds (64 per cent) of offenders were linked to these establishments. Nearly two-thirds (63 per cent) displayed at least one indicator of organised crime.

Commercial parlours

14 brothels advertised as legitimate businesses offering massage services, but with a clear indication they were brothels operating in plain sight. They were well known to police due to their relatively stable and overt presence on high streets. Nearly half of the known off-street sex workers (47 per cent) and approaching a third (30 per cent) of offenders were linked to commercial parlours, and all displayed at least one indicator of organised crime.

Pop-up brothels

13 were temporary brothels which established themselves for short periods of time (sometimes days) in

1 HM Government (2013) Serious and Organised Crime Strategy. London: TSO.

2 Mills, H., Skodbo, S. and Blyth, P. (2013) Understanding organised crime: Estimating the scale and the social and economic costs. London: Home Office.

3 In terms of the definition for organised crime in the HM Government Serious and Organised Crime Strategy (2013).

4 HM Government (2013) Serious and Organised Crime Strategy. London: TSO.

hotels or short-term apartment lets in the city. Nearly all displayed at least one indicator of organised crime, most commonly the movement of sex workers between brothels.

Practitioners knew the least about pop-up brothels but considered them to present the greatest threat of trafficking. Their transient nature meant many did not come to the attention of the police so they are likely to have been much more prevalent than was indicated in police records. In all types of brothel there was a high degree of turnover, with few sex workers staying in one establishment for long; one brothel employing Chinese nationals saw new sex workers arriving every week. This, along with a limited understanding of how the market operates (for example, how sex workers are recruited), made it difficult to develop a clear intelligence picture and assess the threat of exploitation.

What's the impact?

To counter the problem of under-reporting, practitioners rely on pre-established indicators to assess the likelihood that a person is being exploited[5]. The analysis presented here applied the same framework to assess places (i.e. each brothel) rather than people, using information recorded in police intelligence. Key findings include:

5 This assessment drew on a framework published by the United Nations International Labour Office (2009) Operational indicators of trafficking in human beings. Geneva: International Labour Office.

⇨ One in five (12 brothels, 18 per cent) had forced, intimidated or coerced women into providing sexual services; this was most evident in residential brothels. Similarly, sex workers from nearly one in five (12 brothels, 18 per cent) had expressed fear or anxiety.

⇨ In a minority of (mostly residential) brothels (eight brothels, 12 per cent), sex workers had reported being debt-bonded.

⇨ Practitioners described debts having been imposed, to cover the costs of travel from their home countries as a common control mechanism used by smugglers or traffickers.

⇨ There were multiple indicators of control or restrictions within the brothels. Approaching one in five (12 brothels, 18 per cent) employed sex workers who were unable to produce passports or other relevant documents, potentially restricting their ability to leave. In nearly a quarter (15 brothels, 23 per cent) the sex workers slept at the premises; in the case of one brothel, sex workers arrived for a number of days and did not leave the premises during their entire stay. There was also evidence of restrictions being placed on movements (eight brothels, 12 per cent) and third parties controlling the online accounts of sex workers on an adult website (seven brothels, 11 per cent).

The most commonly recorded nationality for known sex workers was Romanian (57 sex workers, 43 per cent); these were the only national group found to be working in pop-up brothels. British nationals made up a minority of sex workers in brothels (22 sex workers, 17 per cent), most of whom had worked in a commercial parlour. The remainder of sex workers were a mix of EU and non-EU nationals. A small number of residential brothels only employed women from an Asian background (one had strong links to Thailand). Consequently, many had few or no ties to the communities in which they were (often temporarily) working, which appeared to marginalise them and impede access to mainstream support services. In interviews, practitioners described how foreign nationals were personally threatened with violence, which could extend to their families at home, thus limiting the capacity of local police and other agencies to safeguard individuals who were understandably concerned for the welfare of themselves and their families.

Unlike the more visible aspects of the sex market that occur on the streets, the exploitation of those working in the off-street sex trade was not seen or experienced by the public to anywhere near the same degree. Where it was visible, practitioners described a tolerance of the off-street sex market within the community. For example, commercial parlours were an accepted feature of some high streets and were populated in the main by itinerant sex workers who were not constituent members of the community. The result was a relative lack of public concern, which limited the pressure on public services to tackle the issue.

September 2016

⇨ The above information is reprinted with kind permission from The Police Foundation. Please visit www.police-foundation.org.uk for further information.

Sex worker unions are reforming their industry

An article from **The Conversation.**

By Gregor Gall, Professor of Industrial Relations, University of Bradford

How best to regulate the sex industry is a frequent topic of discussion. But most of it focuses on moves by governments to criminalise people who pay for sex. France, for example, has recently joined a long list of countries, including Sweden, Iceland, Norway and Northern Ireland, in making it illegal to purchase a sexual service.

Yet this runs contrary to the views of many who work in the industry. If their voices were listened to, we might see a very different approach to regulating sex work.

In France, as with these other countries, the representatives of sex workers have campaigned against the introduction of criminalisation. They believe it endangers the safety of sex workers, as the selling of sex will continue but be driven underground. Their slogan is "nothing about us without us". In other words, no policy should be devised or action taken concerning sex work without the full and direct participation of the workers involved and their representatives.

Forming labour unions is one of the main ways that sex workers are attempting to challenge the way the industry they work in is regulated. Sex worker activists en masse favour decriminalisation and a large number have sought to create a representative body to campaign for it.

> **"In France, as with these other countries, the representatives of sex workers have campaigned against the introduction of criminalisation. They believe it endangers the safety of sex workers, as the selling of sex will continue but be driven underground"**

Like any other work

The unionisation of sex workers typifies many of the sharpest challenges for groups trying to unionise. These include organising self-employed workers with no regular or fixed place of work, high levels of turnover and, effectively, zero hour contracts – all within greatly expanding labour markets due to migration. However, unlike any other workers, sex workers also face moral opprobrium from both within and outside of the labour union movement as a result of the work they do. So there is an additional hurdle to be overcome in the process of unionisation.

Yet, despite these challenges, sex worker activists have succeeded in persuading fellow workers to unionise (either through joining existing unions or creating new ones) in 30 countries including the US, UK, India and Cambodia. They have been spurred on by the realisation that sex work is work much like any other, and that sex workers need and want rights.

Sex workers have problems in common with other workers such as lack of holiday pay, fines for bogus infractions at work, being compelled to do unpaid overtime, bullying by managers and being forced to work long hours without breaks. But there are also different problems which most workers don't have to face such as having to pay fees to work and purchasing work items from their bosses. From both, a sense of injustice and an array of grievances have developed.

Added to their discontent over these issues, sex workers also want to add a political voice to their economic one. Consequently, they have used unionisation to amplify their public position on the legal status of sex work.

"Sex workers have problems in common with other workers such as lack of holiday pay, fines for bogus infractions at work, being compelled to do unpaid overtime, bullying by managers and being forced to work long hours without breaks"

No easy task

But unionisation has been no easy task. The numbers involved have been small, progress has been limited in making substantive gains, and many organisations have folded such as the Red Thread union in The Netherlands. Notable highlights have been collective bargaining over contracts for terms and conditions of work (remuneration, working hours, grievance and discipline procedures and so on), as well as individual and wider political representation.

Formal collective bargaining has taken place in Australia, Britain, Germany and the US, while individual representation has also taken place through the sex work establishments' grievance procedures as well as through legal action in many more countries. Political representation has involved campaigning and lobbying to reform the legal regulation of sex work. Informal collective bargaining, assisted by legal recourse, has also taken place, especially with regard to fees levied to work for exotic dancers and their campaign to be accorded employed status in the US.

After initial successes, energy levels have waned. Organisational development has stalled and many sex worker unions have folded. Along the way, there have been some almighty and bitter internal disputes among sex workers over whether managers should be members and which groups of sex workers (for example, men, women or transgender) should be prioritised over others.

Yet, despite these problems, when one organisation has folded another has often emerged to take its place and carry on the battle for representation. This demonstrates the continuing demand for collective interest representation and the willingness of activists to step up to the plate to provide that representation. Sex worker unionisation is therefore very much a work in progress and a battle still being fought across the world.

My research suggests that developing an occupational form of labour unionism is the best way forward. This means instead of trying to gain bargaining rights in each individual sex work establishment, which is an arduous process, sex workers would seek to regulate their industry as a whole by controlling the standards and practices within it, as well as who has entry to it. One way to do this is through creating a sense of industry identity, at the same time as organising themselves through their union. It will be a difficult task but potentially more rewarding in the long run.

12 May 2016

⇨ The above information is reprinted with kind permission from *The Conversation*. Please visit www.theconversation.com for further information.

Sex workers' rights: mapping policy around the world

The creator of a global map of sex work law hopes the new tool will help tackle decades of myths and misinformation.

By Cheryl Overs

A map that brings together all the laws relating to sex work around the globe has been a long time coming.

After decades of working on sex work issues, I have for some time been frustrated at the lack of accurate and accessible information about laws and policies governing how sex is bought and sold across the world. Without this it is impossible to fully understand how these laws impact on human rights, economic outcomes, gender-based violence, public health or human trafficking. In other words, we cannot enable sex workers to live and work safely.

Unsurprisingly, without the correct information, myths abound and debates become polarised. This was illustrated by the recent reactions to Amnesty International's endorsement of decriminalising sex work. What also became clear was that although we have invented many ways to describe the various legal approaches to sex work – prohibition, regulation, toleration, decriminalisation, legalisation, depenalisation and partial decriminalisation to name a few – there is no consensus about what these terms actually mean. And more to the point – they don't appear in any legal texts.

Laws clearly affect sex workers when they are arrested or required to undergo medical examinations. But they also affect them indirectly by shaping the sex industry and its working conditions, and ultimately by forming a barrier to citizenship and the ability to claim rights.

So what does the Global Sex Work Law Map tell us, and how can activists, researchers and policymakers use it? The map contains country by country accounts of law and policy that directly address female sex workers and the sex industry. There is also a search function that shows groups of countries with similar features, such as where sex workers are forcibly tested for STIs and HIV, and which countries conflate trafficking and sex work by deeming consent to be irrelevant.

The map reveals several interesting trends and patterns. For example, of the 11 legal approaches set out, the one that illuminates most space across the world map is "illegal to solicit to sell sex in a public place and to organise commercial sex in any place". This means that much of the heterosexual commercial sex taking place globally is criminalised by laws against third parties such as brothel managers rather than by laws against the women who sell sex.

Perhaps most surprising is that in many countries sex work is not criminalised by law that mentions prostitution, but by less defined laws against vagrancy, loitering, immorality and debauchery. This information is crucial because it tells us that reform must go further than merely removing the law against selling sex. To end violence and extortion of sex workers and enable them to access justice, services and decent work conditions requires new, location-specific legal and regulatory frameworks as well as fresh approaches to health, economic programmes and cultural change.

Of course the map has its limitations. It only contains the laws that affect women who sell sex – a different stream of law affects male sex workers. Sources were more reliable for some countries than others and definitions vary enormously. For example, some countries define a brothel as any place a sex worker lives or works. In other countries it is a place where sex is sold by more than one woman. In some countries laws address transwomen but in others it applies only to those designated female at birth. For these reasons we designed the map so it can be refined with inputs from users.

As the dust settles after the debates set off by Amnesty's decision to support the decriminalisation of sex work it is clear that, for all the differences of opinion, there is a genuine appetite to solve problems associated with sex work and broad recognition that criminalisation fails to do that. At national and sub-national level, the challenge is to develop concrete, feasible ideas for effective laws and policies. This requires drilling down past big claims and moral arguments, past activists' slogans and sensationalist headlines, and into the details of laws and policies and how they are enforced in different cultural, political, social and economic environments. I am confident that the Sex Work Law Map will be an important tool in that process.

15 September 2015

⇨ The above information is reprinted with kind permission from *The Guardian*. Please visit www.theguardian.com for further information.

A soldier and a sex worker walk into a therapist's office. Who's more likely to have PTSD?

THE CONVERSATION

An article from **The Conversation.**

By Mary-Anne Kate, PhD Candidate in Psychology, University of New England and Graham Jamieson, Senior Lecturer, School of Behavioural, Cognitive and Social Sciences, University of New England

When we think about post-traumatic stress disorder (PTSD), we most often think of soldiers traumatised by their experiences of war. But the statistics tell another story.

While about 5–12% of Australian military personnel who have experienced active service have PTSD at any one time, this is about the same (10%) as rates for police, ambulance personnel, firefighters and other rescue workers.

And while these rates are significant, they are not vastly different to rates in the general Australian population (8% of women and 5% of men).

PTSD is actually most common in populations with a high exposure to forms of complex trauma. This involves multiple, chronic and deliberately inflicted interpersonal traumas (physical and sexual abuse and assaults, emotional abuse, neglect, persecution and torture).

Sex workers, women fleeing domestic violence, survivors of childhood abuse and Indigenous Australians are far more likely to have experienced this complex trauma. In these groups, between 40% and 55% are affected by PTSD.

So, how and why does their complex trauma differ from the PTSD we most commonly associate with the military?

PTSD vs complex PTSD

Complex trauma leads to a specific type of PTSD, known as complex PTSD, which will be listed in the 2018 edition of International Classification of Diseases for the first time.

Complex PTSD applies to responses to extremely threatening or horrific events that are extreme, prolonged or repetitive, from which a person finds it difficult or impossible to escape. Examples include repeated childhood sexual or physical abuse, and prolonged domestic violence.

Generally, PTSD involves persistent mental and emotional stress as a result of injury or severe psychological shock. It typically involves disturbed sleep, traumatic flashbacks and dulled responses to others and the outside world.

But people with complex PTSD also have problems regulating their emotions, believe they are worthless, have deep feelings of shame, guilt or failure, and have ongoing difficulties sustaining relationships and feeling close to others.

Early trauma

Complex PTSD is linked to early trauma, such as childhood physical and sexual abuse. And given girls are two to three times more likely to be sexually abused than boys, this might partly explain why, by the time girls reach adolescence, they are three-and-a-half times more likely than boys to be diagnosed with PTSD. Girls' nervous systems may also be more vulnerable to developing PTSD.

Complex trauma as a child also increases the risk of trauma as an adult. Other studies confirm a link between early trauma and being a victim of domestic violence.

An occupational hazard

People with certain occupations are also at high risk of PTSD. A study of street-based sex workers in Sydney

found nearly half would have met the criteria for a PTSD diagnosis at some point during their lives, making this the highest occupational risk for PTSD in Australia. Their high rates of PTSD are attributed to multiple traumas, including childhood sexual abuse and violent physical or sexual assaults while working.

People with histories of complex trauma are also more likely to find work where trauma is an occupational hazard, like the military or police, with the potential to compound their trauma further.

People with histories of childhood abuse and other adverse childhood experiences are also more likely to develop PTSD in the line of duty.

Other groups at risk

Women fleeing domestic violence are at particular risk of PTSD, with an Australian study finding 42% of women in a women's refuge suffering from it.

While domestic violence is a form of complex trauma in itself, it is far more likely to be experienced by women who, as children, experienced sexual abuse, severe beatings by parents, and who were also raised in homes with domestic violence. These experiences of complex trauma in childhood and adulthood significantly increase the risk of having complex PTSD in adulthood.

Another of the most at-risk groups is Indigenous Australians, with a study in a remote community finding 97% had experienced traumatic events and 55% met the criteria for PTSD at some point in their lives.

Indigenous Australians have high rates of interpersonal trauma that frequently begin early in life and are characterised as severe, chronic and perpetrated by multiple people, often those in authority and well known to the individual. These complex traumas are further compounded by the pervasive transgenerational impacts of colonisation.

Stigma remains

PTSD in the military, police and emergency services in the line of duty has less stigma attached to it than PTSD associated with domestic violence situations and sex workers, partly because some people think this last group created the problem themselves.

Such misconceptions reflect a lack of awareness about the impact of complex trauma on a person's self-worth, coping skills and ability to gauge danger, then effectively respond to it.

Survivors of complex trauma are less likely to be treated for their PTSD despite their symptoms being more pervasive.

This may not be surprising given survivors of complex trauma are often faced with societal, community and family pressure to remain silent, and have a legitimate fear of being accused of fantasising, lying, seeking attention or seeking revenge.

And without adequate professional support, many survivors of complex trauma self-medicate with drugs and alcohol.

Engaging with the healthcare system

There are pitfalls for people with complex PTSD who engage with the mental health care system. This is because the standard treatment for PTSD, exposure therapy, which involves talking about their experience and their reaction to it, can be potentially retraumatising and destabilising. Healthcare professionals might also miss the underlying trauma if the focus is on more visible symptoms, like substance abuse, depression or anxiety.

But the new diagnostic category of complex PTSD provides an opportunity to screen high-risk populations that would be unlikely to seek treatment.

The new diagnostic category also allows treatments to sensitively address standard PTSD symptoms as well as the emotional dysregulation, negative self-perceptions and relationship disturbances that come with it.

27 March 2018

⇨ The above information is reprinted with kind permission from *The Conversation*. Please visit www.theconversation.com for further information.

Commercial sexual exploitation

What is commercial sexual exploitation?

Commercial sexual exploitation (CSE) includes sexual activities which objectify and harm others (usually women) such as prostitution, phone sex, stripping Internet sex/chat rooms, pole dancing, lap dancing, peep shows, pornography, trafficking, sex tourism and mail-order brides.

The Scottish Government includes prostitution, pornography and other forms of involvement in the 'sex industry' in its definition of violence against women. It considers that the exploitation of women through these forms of 'entertainment' legitimises negative attitudes towards women and is inextricably linked to gender inequality and sexual violence.

Who is at risk?

The key risk factor for experiencing CSE is being female.

Commercial sexual exploitation can happen to both women and men. Women involved are often on low incomes, are substance users and there is strong evidence that they have experience of other forms of gender-based violence.

It is difficult to quantify the numbers of women involved in commercial sexual exploitation, partly because some activities, such as pole dancing, are seen as 'normal' and others, such as trafficking into prostitution, are criminal and hidden.

Although much fewer men are involved in prostitution than women, the evidence suggests that those involved become so for reasons similar to women, i.e. lack of options available, previous experience of abuse, drug misuse and homelessness.

Health impact

Commercial sexual exploitation adversely affects physical, sexual and mental health and is a serious public health issue.

The health impact of CSE can be profound, both as a result of coping with the consequences of exploitation and because of the greater exposure to violence and other forms of abuse inherent in this activity.

Some of the signs to look out for include:

⇨ Substance misuse

⇨ Headaches, fatigue, dizzy spells and back pain

⇨ Depression, anxiety, hostility, dissociation and signs of post-traumatic stress disorder

⇨ Suicidality

⇨ Signs of physical assault

⇨ Signs of rape and sexual assault

⇨ HIV, STIs and urinary tract infections

⇨ Repeated terminations of pregnancy.

Other factors may alert you to the possibility of commercial sexual exploitation:

⇨ Difficulty in getting to health services during normal working hours

⇨ Inability to keep appointments (through drug addiction/intoxication)

⇨ Lack of money to travel to appointments or pay for prescriptions

⇨ Disclosure of child sexual abuse or domestic abuse

⇨ Homelessness

⇨ Evidence to suggest control or domination by a partner or pimp.

⇨ The above information is reprinted with kind permission from NHS Scotland. Please visit www.gbv.scot.nhs.uk for further information.

© Scotland's Health on the Web 2017

Porn blocking legislation to cement Internet filtering in UK law

By Cara McGoogan

Forthcoming Internet legislation will enshrine the rights of Internet providers to block pornography websites into law, bypassing EU rules that prevent online content being filtered.

The move, which is part of a wider crackdown on online porn, represents a threat to EU "net neutrality" laws that protect a free and open Internet.

It has been added as a proposal in the Digital Economy Bill, which has passed the House of Commons and spells out the Government's plans to block explicit websites that don't employ strict age verification.

An amendment to the Bill tabled this week hands Internet service providers [ISPs] such as BT the power to filter websites that could be harmful.

ISPs already filter content, requiring users to opt out if they want to access adult websites. But if the Bill passes with the amendment it will be the first legislation in the UK regarding Internet filters, ratifying blocks ISPs have already put in place for "child protection or other purposes".

"It's certainly the first time that the UK has said ISPs can filter but the reality is that ISPs have been doing this for some time," said Neil Brown, an Internet and telecoms lawyer at decode:Legal. "The intention is to ensure ISPs can continue their filtering."

The Government said it follows the policy started by David Cameron and continued by Theresa May of introducing strict measures to keep children safe online.

"We are committed to keeping children safe from harmful pornographic content on the Internet and this amendment will give Internet service providers reassurance the family friendly filters they currently offer are compliant with EU law," said a spokesman for the Department of Culture, Media and Sport.

But some say that such restrictions contravene the EU's "net neutrality" law, which prevents Internet providers from interfering with online traffic. Although the UK opted out of this law for porn blocking after it was passed in 2015 the right to block websites had not been enshrined in the law.

"Some people have certainly said that ISPs shouldn't be doing this but so far [communications regulator] Ofcom hasn't said that they have to stop," Mr Brown said.

The Internet Service Providers Association said it was in favour of the amendment and the added protection it will offer children.

"The amendment protects the status quo around parental control features, which have been in place without legislation," said a spokesman. "It gives a little bit more certainty to people that have the illusion that such filters are against net neutrality.

"We are committed to working with our members to raising the issue of safety more broadly and helping parents protect their children and teenagers."

Critics say a truly open internet should have no blocks at all. "Our research has shown that filters incorrectly blocked tens of thousands of websites including charities, blogs and businesses. They also fail to block some adult content,"

said Pam Cowburn, communications director for the Open Rights Group.

"It's important that ISPs get consent from their customers before switching them on so that parents are aware of their limitations," she added. At the moment most ISPs automatically filter content and customers have to opt out to stop them.

The Bill, which passed in the House of Commons at the end of last year, has been controversial since it will require pornography websites that don't conduct age verification checks on visitors to be blocked. A UN official warned this could be a breach of human rights for failing to protect the right to freedom of opinion and expression.

The Government insists it will protect children online, with research showing 53% of those aged 11 to 16 have encountered pornographic material online.

These vital filters allow parents to protect children from this content, which we know they do accidentally stumble upon and can upset or confuse them," said an NSPCC spokesman.

"We welcome the legislation as it will help ensure that UK parents and children can continue to filter adult, and potentially harmful, content in their homes and keep young people safe and happy online."

26 January 2017

⇨ The above information is reprinted with kind permission from *The Telegraph*. Please visit www.telegraph.co.uk for further information.

Pornography filter, attitudes to pornography

The graphs below demonstrate the results of a YouGov survey investigating public attitudes to pornography and whether pornography filters should be included on all Internet accounts.

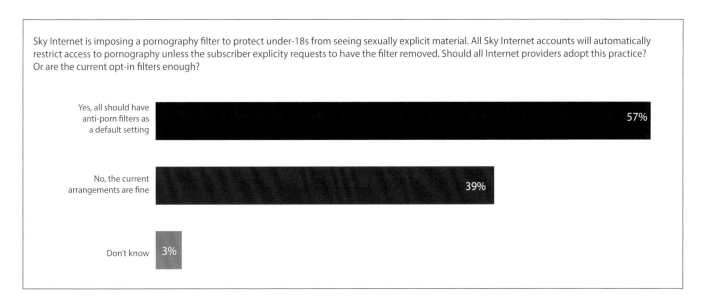

Sky Internet is imposing a pornography filter to protect under-18s from seeing sexually explicit material. All Sky Internet accounts will automatically restrict access to pornography unless the subscriber explicity requests to have the filter removed. Should all Internet providers adopt this practice? Or are the current opt-in filters enough?

- Yes, all should have anti-porn filters as a default setting — **57%**
- No, the current arrangements are fine — **39%**
- Don't know — **3%**

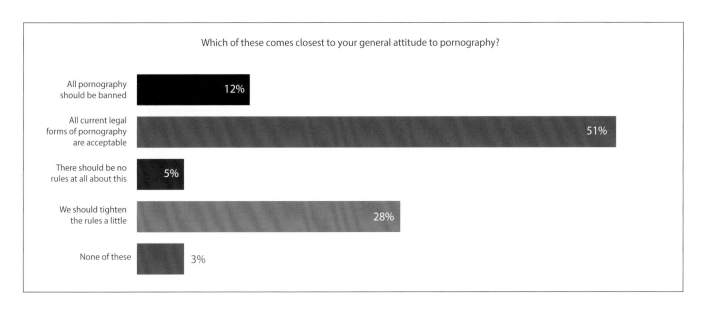

Which of these comes closest to your general attitude to pornography?

- All pornography should be banned — **12%**
- All current legal forms of pornography are acceptable — **51%**
- There should be no rules at all about this — **5%**
- We should tighten the rules a little — **28%**
- None of these — **3%**

Source: YouGov 2015

Online porn

Advice on how to talk to your child about the risks of online porn and sexually explicit material.

Children and young people are now able to access porn online very easily. Whether by accident – website popups and misleading links, or because they are actively looking, it's important for us to help young people understand the impact porn can have on them and their relationships.

As a parent, it is important to understand the risks associated with watching porn at a young age so that you can talk to your child about how to stay safe and what to do if they ever feel concerned or uncomfortable about something they've seen.

It is normal for young people to be curious about sex and relationships. The Internet gives them a way to access information and get answers to questions they may feel uncomfortable about asking you. We know that there are a number of other reasons young people may be accessing porn online.

How to talk to your child about porn

Talking to your child about online porn is something that you may find challenging but it's important to be open and honest.

Finding the right time to talk to your child about porn can be tricky but you know your child best and will know when it's the right time to have these conversations.

Things to talk about

Feeling embarrassed

Acknowledge that your child might feel embarrassed or worried about talking to you. Reassure them that it is ok to feel curious about sex and that they can always talk to you. Remember that they may have seen something online by accident or been pressured to look/watch by another person or group.

Online porn isn't real

Explain that sex in porn is often different to how people have sex in real life. People are acting and putting on a performance so things are exaggerated and the lines between consent, pleasure and violence are often blurred. It's important for young people to know the difference.

Talking about healthy relationships can be a way of pointing out the differences between how actors and actresses in porn interact and how we do in our day-to-day lives.

Healthy relationships

It is important for your child to understand that relationships they see in porn are very different, often not realistic, compared to real relationships.

Talk to them about what makes a positive and healthy relationship Ask them what they think makes a good relationship. You can prompt them by discussing respect, personal boundaries and consent. This conversation may vary depending on your child's age.

Porn addiction

There is a growing body of research looking into the impact that porn has on the brain. Watching porn can become "a high" similar to the way addicts feel when they take drugs (Voon et al, 2014). Scientists are discovering that excessive porn use can have a negative impact on key parts of the brain (Kühn and Gallinat, 2014). For children and young people, these effects can be greater as their brains are still developing (Voon et al, 2014).

Not everyone watches porn

Sometimes children and young people feel pressured to watch porn. Explain to your child that whilst some people watch porn online, not everyone does and it's definitely not something they have to.

Let them know it's OK not to want to watch or do something that makes them feel uncomfortable and they should never be pressured or forced into anything. Explain why you think that online porn may be inappropriate for them. Use reference points – news stories or tv shows – as a way to frame the discussion.

Safe places to get information about sex and relationships

If you feel that there are some things about sex and relationships that your child would feel uncomfortable talking to you about, there are safe places online where they can get information.

ChildLine – the website provides young people with information and advice about online porn. The information is for young people aged 12 and above and aims to answer any difficult questions or concerns they may have.

Think U Know – offers age-appropriate advice for young people, with content broken down from ages five to seven up to 14+. They also have content for parents and other adults responsible for the well being of children.

Brook – the UK's largest young people's sexual health charity. For 50 years, Brook has been providing sexual health services, support and advice to young people under the age of 25.

BBC Advice – helps young people with a broad range of issues. The information on the site is based on advice from medical professionals, government bodies, charities and other relevant groups.

The Site – content on The Site is aimed at young people aged 16+. They offer "real world" advice on a range of subjects including sex and relationships, drink and drugs, and health.

Risks of online porn to children and young people

Childline has seen a 6% increase in counselling sessions where the young person specifically mentioned concerns about online porn or websites containing harmful content (NSPCC, 2015). Concerns related to addiction and worries about forming relationships in the future:

"I'm always watching porn and some of it is quite aggressive. I didn't think it was affecting me at first but I've started to view girls a bit differently recently and it's making me worried. I would like to get married in the future but I'm scared it might never happen if I carry on thinking about girls the way I do."

Boy, 12-15

Studies have also shown that when children and young people are exposed to sexually explicit material, they are at greater risk of developing:

⇨ unrealistic attitudes about sex and consent

⇨ more negative attitudes towards roles and identities in relationships

⇨ more casual attitudes towards sex and sexual relationships

⇨ an increase in 'risky' sexual behaviour

⇨ unrealistic expectations of body image and performance.

The impact that porn can have on a young person depends on a number of factors, including:

⇨ the age and gender of the child

⇨ the type of porn that is being viewed

⇨ how often they are watching porn

⇨ what their relationships are like at home and with their friends

⇨ existing beliefs and values on sex and relationships

What the law says

You can legally buy porn magazines and videos at 18, and all regulated porn websites try to prevent under 18s from accessing them. The government has recently clarified existing obscenity laws to ensure that materials rated only suitable for 18-year-olds (and above) have controls in place to stop children under 18 from accessing them.

There are certain types of porn that are illegal – even for an adult to be in possession of. These are called "extreme pornographic images", and include acts that threaten a person's life, acts which are likely to, or, result in serious injury, degrading porn, violent porn (which includes rape and abuse) or anything involving those under the age of 18.

It is illegal for a person under 18 to send explicit images or films of themselves, or of another young person. By sending an explicit image, a young person is producing and distributing child abuse images and risks being prosecuted, even if the picture is taken and shared with their permission.

References

Häggström-Nordin, E., Sandberg, J., Hanson, U. and Tydén, T. (2006) 'It's everywhere!' young Swedish people's thoughts and reflections about pornography. *Scandinavian Journal of Caring Science*, 20(4): 386–393.

Häggström-Nordin E., Tydén T., Hanson U., et al. (2009) Experiences of and attitudes towards pornography among a group of Swedish high school students. *European Journal of Contraception and Reproductive Health Care*, 14(4): 277–284.

Horvarth, M.A.H., Alys, L., Massey, K., Pina, A., Scally, M. and Adler, J.R. (2013) 'Basically... porn is everywhere': a rapid evidence assessment on the effect that access and exposure to pornography has on children and young people (PDF). [London]: Office of the Children's Commissioner (OCC).

Lofgren-Mårtenson, L., and Månsson, S.A. (2010) Lust, love, and life: a qualitative study of Swedish adolescents' perceptions and experiences with pornography. *Journal of Sex Research*, 47(6): 568-579.

Mattebo, M., Tydén, T., Häggström-Nordin, E., Nilsson, K.W. and Larsson, M. (2013) Pornography consumption, sexual experiences, lifestyles, and self-rated health among male adolescents in Sweden. *Journal of Developmental and Behavioural Pediatrics*, 34(7): 460-468.

⇨ The above information is reprinted with kind permission from the NSPCC. Please visit www.nspcc.co.uk for further information.

"I wasn't sure it was normal to watch it…"

An extract from the report by NSPCC, Children's Commissioner and Middlesex University London.

1.2 Key findings

1.2.1 Which children reported seeing pornography?

Who has seen online pornography?

⇨ More boys view online pornography, through choice, than girls;

⇨ At 11, the majority of children had not seen online pornography (28% of 11-12 year olds report seeing pornography);

⇨ By 15, children were more likely than not to have seen online pornography (65% of 15-16 year olds report seeing pornography);

⇨ Children were as likely to stumble across pornography as to search for it deliberately.

1. Just under half of the stage two sample reported never having seen online pornography, they were more likely to be younger and female;

2. Just over half of the stage two sample had been exposed to online pornography by the age of 16 and of those who had seen it, 94% reported seeing it by age 14;

3. Of those who were still seeing online pornography, 46% (476) reported searching for it actively;

4. Young people were as likely to find pornography by accident as to find it deliberately;

5. Greater proportions of boys see online pornography than the proportions of girls who see it – this is whether deliberately or accidentally;

6. Boys continue seeing pornography, more often and more deliberately than girls;

7. Older children are more likely to see pornography, more often, than younger children, whether deliberately or accidentally.

1.2.2 Feelings and attitudes towards online pornography

What do young people say that they feel?

⇨ On first viewing pornography, young people report a mixture of emotions, including curiosity, shock and confusion;

⇨ Shock and confusion subsides on repeated viewing, whether pornography is deliberately sought out, or accidentally viewed;

⇨ Younger children were less likely to engage with online pornography critically than older children and were more likely to report feeling disturbed by what they have seen.

1. Girls are more negative about pornography than boys;

2. Of the stage two participants who answered the question, a greater proportion of boys (53%) reported pornography was realistic than the proportion of girls (39%);

3. A minority of respondents reported sexual arousal on first viewing pornography (17%), rising to 49% at current viewing;

4. Older respondents (15–16-year-olds) who chose to view online pornography predominantly reported doing so for pleasure;

5. Some of the respondents felt curious (41%), shocked (27%) or confused (24%) on first viewing pornography;

6. The negative feelings subsided through repeated viewing of online pornography. When asked about how they now feel about online pornography that they still view, 30% reported that they remained curious (initially 41%), 8% remained shocked (down from 27%), and 4% remained confused (down from 24%);

7. When asked to rate their overall attitudes towards pornography, mixed responses included that it was unrealistic (49%), arousing (47%), exciting (40%), silly (36%), exploitative (38%) and scary (23%);

Some of these attitudes varied by age and gender with more boys being more positive, particularly in older age groups.

1.2.3 Risks and harms

Some older children want to act out the pornography they have seen.

⇨ Substantial minorities of older children wanted to try things out they had seen in pornography;

⇨ A greater proportion of boys wanted to emulate pornography than the proportions of girls;

⇨ Pornographic material has been received by a quarter of the sample;

⇨ A minority of young people had generated naked or semi-naked images of themselves; some of them had shared the images further.

1. Most young people in the stage two sample had not wanted to emulate anything that they had seen in pornography. However, substantial minorities did report that online pornography has given them ideas that they wanted to try out;

2. The proportions wishing to emulate pornography increase with age – 21% for 11-–2 year olds; 39% for the 13–14 year olds and 42% for the 15–16 year olds;

3. Some 44% of males, compared to 29% of females, reported that the online pornography they had seen had given them ideas about the types of sex they wanted to try out;

4. 26% of surveyed respondents had received online pornography or links to it and 4% reported

sending others pornography online, or links to it.

1.2.4 'Sexting'

Young people's definition of 'sexting' is textual, not visual.

⇨ The vast majority of young people had not taken naked selfies;

⇨ Just over half of those who had taken intimate selfies had shared them with others, these are mainly, but not always, people they know;

⇨ There was limited knowledge of how to remove online images of themselves.

1. None of the children in focus groups described sexting as taking and sharing self-generated photographs of naked bodies or body parts. Rather, they interpreted sexting as writing and sharing sexually explicit or intimate words to people they knew, normally their boyfriend or girlfriend;

2. The vast majority of survey respondents did not report having taken naked 'selfies', however:

   • 123 young people (12% of the respondents) had taken topless pictures of themselves (88 boys, 33 girls and two young people who did not identify in a gender binary way);

   • 41 (4%) had taken pictures of themselves that showed their "bottom half naked" (26 boys, 14 girls and 1 young person who did not identify in a gender binary way);

   • 27 (3%) had taken fully naked pictures of themselves (13 boys, 13 girls and one young person who did not identify in a gender binary way);

3. In total, 135 young people (14%) had taken naked, and, or, semi-naked images of themselves. Just over half of them went on to share the images with others (i.e. 7% of the survey participants shared images). 49 of them had been

asked to share their pictures online:

   • Most boys who had shared their images reported not being asked to share the pictures, (67 out of 96 boys who had generated and shared such images). Conversely, most girls who generated and shared naked or semi-naked images reported that they **had** been asked to share the pictures with someone (22/37), this difference may have implications for intervention;

   • The majority of respondents (30/49) who had taken and shared naked or semi-naked self-images online, reported that they knew the person they showed them to;

   • This leaves some who did not know the people with whom they shared intimate images of themselves, this was a matter considered in terms of child protection and safeguarding;

   • 25 young people said that they had shared images of themselves performing a sexual act (12 boys, 12 girls and one young person who did not identify in a gender binary way);

4. During the stage three online focus groups, all participants were asked: "Would you be able to remove an intimate image of yourself or would you need to get help? (E.g. ChildLine/IWF partnership)". Only the older children (15-16) knew about this possibility and all age groups felt that not enough information was available to children and young people;

5. Very few young people said they had:

   • created a fully-naked image of others –11/948 who answered the question (1% of all respondents);

   • taken top-half naked pictures of someone else – 34/948 who answered the question (3% of the whole sample);

   • taken pictures of someone else, naked from the waist down – 13/948 answering

the question (1% of all respondents).

1.2.5 Young people as critical users of pornography

How do young people rate pornography?

⇨ Most young people saw pornography as unrealistic; however, a minority rated it positively;

⇨ More positive responses came from boys, younger respondents and those whose families and/or schools had not engaged with them about online pornography;

⇨ Most young people thought pornography was a poor model for consent or safe sex and wanted better sex education, covering the impact of pornography.

1. As already noted, when reflecting back on their first encounter with online pornography, young people tended to be negative, reporting shock, shame, disgust, but also, curiosity;

2. Those who continued to view pornography tended to shift in their attitudes with lower percentages reporting negative feelings after continued exposure;

3. Young people's assessments of pornography varied. At least three quarters of the stage two sample who had seen pornography (across ages and genders) felt that pornography was a poor model for consent or for safe sex. However, as also noted above, just over half the sample of boys saw pornography as realistic;

4. A few young people agreed that pornography had taught them about the roles that men and women could play in sexual relationships:

   • The majority of young people disagreed with such statements but boys, particularly younger boys, were the group from whom the most positive assessments of pornography were reported;

- The main body of this paper considers what young people may be learning about sexual relationships and gender from pornography and how greater viewing of pornography, whether deliberate and accidental, might influence their behaviours;

5. Respondents from the online focus groups suggested that formal school education on the issues surrounding online pornography may help to challenge harmful attitudes towards women, or towards potentially harmful sexual relationships that can stem from exposure to online pornography;

6. Survey data indicated that young people have mixed experiences of PSHE classes. There is some evidence that more sex and relationship education and/ or education about online pornography, may help young people disentangle the competing emotions they experience when viewing pornography online;

7. Survey data also indicate that if young people have seen troubling material, it may help to have a parent to talk to, but the findings are somewhat equivocal;

8. Young people were creative and often enthusiastic about potential opportunities to improve their learning about sex and relationships and online interactions.

June 2016

⇨ The above information is reprinted with kind permission from the NSPCC, the Office for Children's Commissioner and Middlesex University London. Please visit mdx.ac.uk for further information.

Woman schools men in sexual consent with analogy about stealing money

"It's disgusting it needs to be said but that was a brilliant way of putting it."

By Natasha Hinde

In this day and age, it's pretty sad that the issue of consent is still a grey area for some. But that's the reality.

According to Rape Crisis, roughly 85,000 women and 12,000 men are raped in England and Wales every year – that's roughly 11 rapes (of adults alone) every hour.

To clear up any confusion that may still arise, Twitter user Nafisa Ahmed, 22, took it upon herself to explain consent by using the analogy of stealing money from a purse.

She wrote: "I don't get how rape is so hard to understand for some men. But, if you put it like this, they get it."

She then shared a series of tweets explaining how consent works in a relatable and super easy to understand concept.

Ahmed said her tweets were in response to comments on her Twitter feed surrounding an incident involving actor and director Nate Parker.

Parker was accused of rape back when he was a student, but was later acquitted in a 2001 trial.

Just this week, it was reported by *Variety* that the woman who had accused Parker of rape had taken her life.

Ahmed said she tweeted about consent after spotting a few tweets on her timeline from a handful of male Twitter users who "came off as 'rape apologists'".

Her tweets were praised on Twitter, with thousands of people sharing them.

One person wrote: "Just saw your tweets on rape. It's disgusting it needs to be said but man that was a brilliant way of putting it."

Others simply thanked Ahmed for sharing her thoughts.

There have been a number of consent analogies shared over the past few years, the most popular of which came from blogger Emmeline May, who likened consent to making a cup of tea.

The idea was later used by Thames Valley Police as part of their #ConsentisEverything campaign.

18 August 2016

⇨ The above information is reprinted with kind permission from The Huffington Post UK. Please visit www.huffingtonpost.co.uk for further information.

nafisa ahmed @thatxxv

If you put a gun to my head to get me to give you $5, you still stole $5. Even if I physically handed you $5.

3:44 PM - 16 Aug 2016

If I let YOU borrow $5, that doesn't give the right for your FRIEND to take $5 out of my purse.

"But you gave him some, why can't I?"

3:44 PM - 16 Aug 2016

If you steal $5 and I can't prove it in court, that does NOT mean you didn't steal $5.

3:45 PM - 16 Aug 2016

Just because I gave you $5 in the past, doesn't mean I have to give you $5 in the future.

3:46 PM - 16 Aug 2016

If you can understand allllllll of that, how do you not understand the concept of rape?

3:46 PM - 16 Aug 2016

"I was kidnapped and sex trafficked in London as a student. It can happen to anybody"

By Cara McGoogan

Frida Farrell was walking towards Oxford Circus one evening when she was approached by a photographer. It was 2002 and Farrell had recently graduated from the Central School of Speech and Drama. In her early 20s and looking for acting work, she was flattered when the photographer said: "We're casting for this project and we saw you walking past and you look perfect."

The photographer was well-dressed and had a nice smile, Farrell remembered. She took his business card and later looked him up online. His story appeared to check out and his website looked professional. So the next day Farrell went to his apartment near Harley Street to have some trial photos taken, including head shots, and some full length ones.

"It was a legit photo shoot," she tells me. And she was pleased when, the next day he called her and said the job was hers if she wanted it. At £7,000 for half a day the offer was hard to refuse.

"I was excited to do a job that would make some quick money, pay the rent," she says.

But when Farrell arrived at the same apartment the following day at noon, things turned sinister. No sooner than she had entered the hall, the nice-looking photographer slammed the door behind her and locked it three times. Then, he pulled out a knife. Farrell felt sick, but knew she had to try and stay calm.

"I would love to say there were loads of things going through my head but there wasn't. There was panic, like, 'How am I going to survive this? What do I need to get through this?'," she says, more than a decade later.

She asked to go to the bathroom and he told her to leave her bag and phone behind. Despite urgently hoping for a way out, the bathroom only had a tiny window that was five storeys above the ground. She wasn't going to be able to escape. Instead she opened the door and decided to play along.

He offered her a glass of milk. "I thought, 'What's worse, the glass of milk or the knife.' So I drank the glass of milk."

Farrell capitulated when the photographer demanded that she put on some underwear and followed his commands to pose for the camera. But she was unable to smile, as he asked, due to the tears that were streaming down her cheeks.

It wasn't long before Farrell blacked out. "He was sitting in a chair and asked me to come over and, you know, 'do things'," she says. "And the next thing I knew I woke up in bed with no clothes on."

After being fed part of a sandwich, Farrell blacked out again and this time woke up in a different apartment. All of the furniture had been stripped from the flat, including the light bulbs and toilet seat. The only item that remained was a wooden-framed bed. For the next three days, men would appear at the apartment and successively rape her, in between the photographer giving her doses of an unknown drug.

After Farrell had been locked in the basement flat near Harley Street for three days, the photographer came into the room in a rush. He told Farrell to get ready as someone was coming, then ran out of the door, forgetting to lock it. Farrell, cautious that it could be a trap, crept towards the door and listened to his footsteps disappearing into the lift.

"I became instantly sober from whatever drugs I had in my body and I slowly opened the door," she explains.

She immediately grabbed some clothes and fled. "I knew there was a doorman in there and I didn't know if he was in on it, but I thought, 'I'm just going to run.' I ran and ran and ran and ran I think for about ten blocks, all the while thinking, 'Is he behind me?'"

She went to stay with a friend, and when she eventually returned to her own flat a week later, she was terrified the photographer would be there. He had told her he knew where she lived.

"I looked behind the shower curtain, I felt ridiculous doing it, like I was in a horror movie," she says. "I'm sure he wouldn't have been there, because why would he bother with one girl who went wrong? He'd just find another one."

Farrell didn't tell anyone about her ordeal for more than a decade, bar her husband and a friend. But now, 14 years later and aged 39, she has decided to open up about it for the first time.

"I was silent about it for so many years. I didn't want to talk about it at all. But then my husband convinced me that I should not only write it down, but write a film to help other women," she says. "Helping other women was more of a drive than being silent about it."

The result is *Selling Isobel*, a feature film directed by Rudolf Buitendach, which recently won the Indie Award at Raindance Film Festival, Britain's biggest independent film festival with a judging panel that included Joanna Lumley and Olivia Colman.

Farrell has only slightly adapted her story for the film, removing some of the most difficult parts "just to make it watchable", and giving the photographer a fictional backstory "to make him a baddie that you can understand".

She decided to play the main character in the film herself, which adds a layer of gravity to the events. "We thought it might be stronger if I played her, and I was ready to do whatever made the story come through in the strongest way," she explains.

Farrell hopes that the film will help young people avoid making similar mistakes to her by realising how at risk they are. "If I say 'imagine a sex trafficking victim', you often think of someone from Eastern Europe who doesn't speak the language. But it can happen to anyone walking down the street. I'm Swedish, but I speak good English and I wasn't struggling for money."

No one knows exactly how many people are sexually exploited in the UK, but estimates suggest thousands of women and men are trafficked into the sex trade in Britain each year. Home Office figures suggest as many as 13,000 people could be living as slaves in the country, with a majority of those working in the sex industry.

Writing in *The Telegraph* less than a fortnight after she took office as prime minister, Theresa May described human slavery as "the greatest human rights issue of our time".

"These crimes must be stopped and the victims of modern slavery must go free," she wrote. "As prime minister I am determined that we will make it a national and international mission to rid our world of this barbaric evil."

As part of her own research into human trafficking in the UK, May said she had met a woman who had come to London to study but was kidnapped and locked in a house in south London, then forced to work as a prostitute by armed captors.

"When she finally escaped to north London, she was picked up by another gang that systematically exploited her and raped many others in a squalid high-street brothel," said May.

Farrell's story shows how at risk young people are, regardless of nationality, proficiency in English and financial means. She was recently walking through London at 2am and she couldn't stop thinking how vulnerable all of the young people on the streets were.

"There were hundreds and hundreds of boys and girls walking on their own and I thought, 'Oh they have no idea how much prey they are.' If they just had a slight awareness of it, they might at least stick with a girlfriend or link arms with a guy friend." Although Farrell has had doubts about whether broadcasting her story in a film was the right thing to do, the reception has affirmed that it was.

"Winning the Raindance award really helped to emphasise that I'm doing the right thing, that I should be talking about it, and other girls should understand it. Other people are in danger that I could help."

After the London screening at the end of September, an 18-year-old girl and her mother approached Farrell. The teenager said she only now realised how naive she had been. An actress herself, the girl said she was often invited into houses alone for readings and auditions. After hearing Farrell's story she said she would always take someone with her. "That was great for me," says Farrell. "I thought, 'Even if it's just that one girl, that's great, job done'."

Farrell has moved on with her life, and is no longer scared – "I don't walk around nervous now." But the photographer was never caught and for Farrell, that is an unnerving thought. As she says: "He might not even be in London now. He could be anywhere."

10 October 2016

⇨ The above information is reprinted with kind permission from *The Telegraph*. Please visit www.telegraph.co.uk for further information.

How Brexit border debate could affect human trafficking into UK

THE CONVERSATION

An article from **The Conversation.**

By Katerina Hadjimatheou, Research Fellow Interdisciplinary Ethics Research Group, University of Warwick and Jennifer Lynch, Early Career Research Fellow, University of Hertfordshire

Recent government figures estimate that there are between 10,000 and 13,000 victims of modern slavery in the UK today. A large majority of these people are trafficked in from abroad. And, as the government report shows, a significant proportion of this group, perhaps even most of them, are themselves EU citizens.

While there is currently great uncertainty about how Brexit will unfold, it seems highly likely that the final settlement will involve some reinstatement of immigration controls between the UK and the EU. So, one important question is how this might affect the flow, identification, and protection of people trafficked into the UK.

Our understanding of the precise role played by migration controls in human trafficking is patchy. This is partly because trafficking is by its nature hard to measure. It's partly because there is, as yet, no systematic research of the sort that would produce reliable evidence. And it's partly because the increasingly politicised nature of the debate confuses an already incomplete picture.

Nevertheless, the need to migrate to escape danger, oppression and/or poverty and the restrictions placed on such migration are generally considered features common to trafficking experiences. For example, in recent years we have seen frequent assertions of a causal connection between tough border controls and increased reliance of people on illegal routes and threatening individuals.

The zealous enforcement of border controls has also been shown to hamper the identification of victims of human trafficking. Under both the Council of Europe's Convention against Trafficking, and the UK's most recent guidance, border forces must be proactive in spotting potential victims at the border.

But the border force's singular focus on enforcing migration controls can make officers blind to indicators of victimhood, including some specific types of behaviour and responses to questioning, as well as interaction with travel partners. Officers looking to exclude as many illegal migrants as possible can end up focusing too much on the credibility of the travellers' stories and not enough on their vulnerability. The consequences of the misidentification of victims of trafficking as illegal migrants can be detention, deportation and re-trafficking.

Safe migration

In light of these concerns, proposals have been voiced for the relaxation of border controls and the establishment of "safe migration" routes. Yet even if the removal of borders were politically achievable, there are reasons to be cautious in our expectations of how that might benefit victims.

Claims about the causal connection between migration control and human trafficking rest on an assumption that those trafficked are nearly always illegal migrants. But this is contradicted by the European experience. EU freedom of movement is the most ambitious border-free experiment of modern times.

However, recent estimates from the European Statistics Agency show that 65% of victims of trafficking registered in the EU are themselves EU citizens. UK records confirm this – in 2014, between half and a third of all recorded victims were EU citizens. This rises to 78% for those exploited for labour.

Politicising the debate

What should we make of this? Some have argued that EU freedom of movement actually facilitates human trafficking within Europe. For example, it is widely recognised that the removal of borders has increased transnational criminal activity including human trafficking. It may also make identification of victims harder at borders. In its 2015 report on modern slavery in the UK, the Centre for Social Justice made this claim:

"Free movement has made it even tougher to spot victims of modern slavery from the EU as they arrive in destination countries legally. This means [European Economic Area] citizens do not come to the attention of either police or immigration and borders agencies."

This is echoed by soon to be published research we carried out in 2015 with border force officers working as anti-trafficking first responders at Heathrow Airport. They reported being required to move EU citizens through the border so quickly that it was almost impossible for them to identify victims.

The conflict between border control and anti-trafficking they describe is not the one referred to typically – namely the risk that victims of trafficking are miscategorised as mere illegal migrants – rather, it is the risk that victims of trafficking are wrongly categorised as legal migrants.

How can we square this with the preceding claims that the implementation of national borders aggravates trafficking? Both may be correct. But attempts to move beyond mere speculation are currently hindered by the politicised nature of the debate. As so often happens with the controversial issue of immigration, arguments are frequently put to the service of preexisting political positions.

For example, it is unsurprising that border force officers, whose professional identity is premised on the need to enforce immigration and customs regulations, would see stricter border controls as an obvious solution to the problem of trafficking. Equally, the Centre for Social Justice is a right-leaning think tank which is sceptical about the benefits of free movement.

On the other hand, "safe migration" routes and similar solutions are typically championed by those who are already troubled by the contribution of migration controls to human suffering.

If we want to be prepared for the changes to come, we need research that can cut through the politics and deliver a much broader, more contextually informed and better evidenced understanding of the drivers of human trafficking into the UK.

14 March 2017

⇨ The above information is reprinted with kind permission from *The Conversation*. Please visit www.theconversation.com for further information.

legal migrants ⟶

police

Key facts

⇨ Whilst most people in prostitution have not been trafficked, many women and children are trafficked to provide sexual services – 62% of all trafficking victims in the EU. (page 1)

⇨ There are approximately 72,800 sex workers in the UK – 88% are women, 6% men and 4% transgender. (page 2)

⇨ Most sex workers are mothers working to support families. 74% of off-street sex workers "cited the need to pay household expenses and support their children." (page 2)

⇨ The average age of entry into prostitution is 19 for women working outdoors and 22 for women working indoors. Claims that the average age of entry into prostitution is 13 years old are based on studies of young people under 18. (page 2)

⇨ Around 11% of British men aged 16–74 have paid for sex on at least one occasion, which equates to 2.3 million individuals. (page 6)

⇨ Sex workers have an average of 25 clients per week paying an average of £78 per visit. (page 6)

⇨ In 2014–15, there were 456 prosecutions of sex workers for loitering and soliciting. (page 6)

⇨ An estimated 152 sex workers were murdered between 1990 and 2015. 49% of sex workers (in one survey) said that they were worried about their safety. (page 6)

⇨ There were 1,139 victims of trafficking for sexual exploitation in 2014 and 248 in April to June 2015 (following implementation of the Modern Slavery Act 2015). (page 6)

⇨ Currently, selling sex is technically legal in Britain; however, restrictions make certain aspects a criminal offence – for example, more than one person at a time selling sex out of a property. (page 13)

⇨ YouGov research finds that most British people (54%) support decriminalising prostitution in Britain, while 21% oppose it. Men have a greater tendency to favour decriminalisation (65–15%), but women do still tend to be in support (43–27%). (page 13)

⇨ Nearly five per cent of UK students have worked in the sex industry and nearly 22 per cent of students have considered working in the sex industry. (page 19)

⇨ In a single city 65 brothels, linked to 74 offenders, were identified over a two-year period. Over three quarters (77 per cent) displayed links to organised crime groups. (page 22)

⇨ The most commonly recorded nationality for known sex workers[is] Romanian (57 sex workers, 43 per cent); these were the only national group found to be working in pop-up brothels. British nationals made up a minority of sex workers in brothels (22 sex workers, 17 per cent), most of whom had worked in a commercial parlour. (page 23)

⇨ Women fleeing domestic violence are at particular risk of PTSD, with an Australian study finding 42% of women in a women's refuge suffering from it.

⇨ 53% of those aged 11 to 16 have encountered pornographic material online. (page 30)

⇨ Studies have also shown that when children and young people are exposed to sexually explicit material, they are at greater risk of developing:

  • unrealistic attitudes about sex and consent

  • more negative attitudes towards roles and identities in relationships

  • more casual attitudes towards sex and sexual relationships

  • an increase in 'risky' sexual behaviour

  • unrealistic expectations of body image and performance. (page 33)

⇨ Childline has seen a 6% increase in counselling sessions where the young person specifically mentioned concerns about online porn or websites containing harmful content (NSPCC, 2015). (page 33)

⇨ At 11, the majority of children have not seen online pornography (28% of 11-12 year olds report seeing pornography). (page 34)

⇨ By 15, children are more likely than not to have seen online pornography (65% of 15-16 year olds report seeing pornography). (page 34)

⇨ 123 young people (12% of the respondents) have taken topless pictures of themselves (88 boys, 33 girls and two young people who did not identify in a gender binary way). (page 35)

⇨ According to Rape Crisis, roughly 85,000 women and 12,000 men are raped in England and Wales every year – that's roughly 11 rapes (of adults alone) every hour. (page 36)

Glossary

Automatic porn filters

Some people feel that automatic porn filters are needed in order to protect people, particularly children, from viewing disturbing pornographic images online. The idea is that, on purchasing a new PC or Internet service, adults would be forced to choose which types of content they wanted to be accessed on their computer. This would mean that any site categorised as inappropriate – sites containing porn, suicide, self-harm sites, etc. – would be blocked. There is concern, however, that this could result in genuine websites being blocked unfairly, for example medical or self-help sites.

Brothel

A house where people can pay to have sex with prostitutes.

Censorship

Banning or cutting out content that is deemed 'unsuitable'. Many people argue that introducing filters to block pornography from Internet searches, would be a form of censorship. Censorship is generally viewed as a negative thing.

Child Sexual Exploitation (CSE)

Using or exploiting a child for sexual purposes. This often goes hand-in-hand with the grooming process and can involve offering the child money, gifts, cigarettes or alcohol in return for sexual favours. CSE can lead to child trafficking and prostitution.

Empower

To give power or authority to someone.

Exploitation

Taking advantage of or using someone for selfish reasons.

Grooming

Actions that are deliberately performed in order to encourage a child to engage in sexual activity. For example, offering friendship and establishing an emotional connection, buying gifts, etc.

Internet Service Provider (ISP)

A company that provides Internet services, such as BT, Talk Talk, Sky, etc.

Pornography

Images or videos that explicitly portray sexual activity.

Prostitution

The exchange of money for sex.

Rape

Forcing someone to engage in sexual intercourse against their will. Force is not necessarily physical, it could also be emotional or psychological.

Sex trafficking

Transporting people from one area to another in order to force them to work in the sex trade – usually as prostitutes, but they could be forced into the porn industry also. Sex trafficking does not just occur between countries, it also happens within the UK and is closely linked to child sexual exploitation and grooming.

Soliciting

When a prostitute searches for clients.

Assignments

Brainstorming

⇨ In small groups, discuss what you know about the sex trade.

- Is prostitution legal in the UK?

- What is sex trafficking?

- What is sexual exploitation?

Research

⇨ In regard to prostitution law, research The Nordic Model – how is it different from complete decriminalisation? Create a fact sheet explaining the basic principles.

⇨ Do some research into the prevalence of prostitution in the Victorian era. What was life like for prostitutes in the 19th century? Have conditions improved for commercial sex workers over the past 150 years? Or are they worse?

⇨ Recreate the YouGov survey from page 13 amongst your class then draw a graph to demonstrate your results.

Design

⇨ Choose one of the articles from this book and create an illustration that highlights the key themes of the piece.

⇨ Design a series of posters and web-banners that will create awareness of sexual exploitation amongst young people.

⇨ Design a poster that illustrates the tweets on page 36, with the aim of highlighting the issue of sexual consent.

⇨ Create an information booklet, to be distributed at your school, explaining sexual exploitation and highlighting the warning signs for young people who might become victims.

⇨ Design a leaflet that gives parents advice about how to talk to their children about pornography. Use the article on page 32 for help.

Oral

⇨ Create an outline for a lesson that will teach pupils from your age group about pornography. Think carefully about what you believe needs to be included in the lesson; which issues are most important? Work in groups and then present back to the rest of your class and compare ideas.

⇨ As a class, stage a television talk show with the theme 'Should we teach pornography in schools?' The talk show panel should include a teacher, a politician, a parent and a journalist. One member of the class should also play the part of the talk show host, fielding questions from the audience as you debate the issue. Take some time to decide who will play each part, and think about what their opinion would be.

⇨ With a partner, discuss the pros and cons of completely legalising prostitution. Make notes and present your ideas back to the class.

Reading/writing

⇨ Write a letter to your MP arguing either for or against an automatic block on Internet porn.

⇨ Write a one paragraph definition of the term human trafficking.

⇨ Read the article Sorry Amnesty, decriminalising sex work will not protect human rights and make a list of the author's key arguments. Share with a partner and see if you've picked out the same points.

⇨ How could the Brexit border debate affect human trafficking in the UK? Write a summary of the article on page 38.

⇨ Imagine that you are an Agony Aunt and you've received a letter from a college student who is worried that her housemate is turning to sex work in order to pay for her living costs while away from home. The housemate is determined that this is a course of action she wishes to take, so what advice would you give the friend? What could she do to help her housemate stay safe?

Acknowledgements

The publisher is grateful for permission to reproduce the material in this book. While every care has been taken to trace and acknowledge copyright, the publisher tenders its apology for any accidental infringement or where copyright has proved untraceable. The publisher would be pleased to come to a suitable arrangement in any such case with the rightful owner.

Images

All images courtesy of iStock except p.11 © Olaia Irigoien, p.15 © Joshua K Jackson, p.18 © Oscar Keys, p.23 © Matthew Sleeper, p.25 © Alessandro Di Credico. Icon on pages 41 and 42 made by Freepik for Flaticon.

Illustrations

Don Hatcher: pages 21 & 28. Simon Kneebone: pages 7 & 33. Angelo Madrid: pages 10 & 39.

Additional acknowledgements

Editorial on behalf of Independence Educational Publishers by Cara Acred.

With thanks to the Independence team: Mary Chapman, Sandra Dennis, Jackie Staines and Jan Sunderland.

Cara Acred

Cambridge, May 2017